D1309242

IMMIGRATION FROM THE MIDDLE EAST

Sheila Smith Noonan

THE CHANGING
Face of North America:
IMMIGRATION SINCE 1965

Asylees

Chinese Immigration

Cuban Immigration

Deported Aliens

Filipino Immigration

Haitian Immigration

Immigration from Central America

Immigration from the Dominican Republic

Immigration from the Former Yugoslavia

Immigration from the Middle East

Immigration from South America

Indian Immigration

Korean Immigration

Mexican Immigration

Refugees

Vietnamese Immigration

IMMIGRATION FROM THE MIDDLE EAST

Sheila Smith Noonan

MASON CREST PUBLISHERS
PHILADELPHIA

LONGWOOD PUBLIC LIBRARY

Produced by OTTN Publishing, Stockton, New Jersey

Mason Crest Publishers
370 Reed Road
Broomall, PA 19008
www.masoncrest.com

Copyright © 2004 by Mason Crest Publishers. All rights reserved.
Printed and bound in the Hashemite Kingdom of Jordan.

First printing

1 3 5 7 9 8 6 4 2

Library of Congress Cataloging-in-Publication Data

Noonan, Sheila Smith.
  Immigration from the Middle East / Sheila Smith Noonan.
      p. cm. — (The changing face of North America)
  Summary: Surveys immigration from the Middle East to the United States
  and Canada since the 1960s, as a result of changes in immigration law.
  Includes bibliographical references and index.
   ISBN 1-59084-695-8
  1. Arab Americans—History—20th century—Juvenile literature. 2. Arabs—Canada—History—20th century—
  Juvenile literature. 3. Iranian Americans—History—20th century—Juvenile literature. 4. Iranians—Canada—
  History—20th century—Juvenile literature. 5. Israelis—United States—History—20th century—Juvenile literature. 6. Israelis—Canada—History—20th century—Juvenile literature. 7. Turkish Americans—History—20th
  century—Juvenile literature. 8. Turks—Canada—History—20th century—Juvenile literature. 9. United States—
  Emigration and immigration—History—20th century—Juvenile literature. 10. Canada—Emigration and immigration—History—20th century—Juvenile literature. 11. Middle East—Emigration and immigration—History—
  20th century—Juvenile literature. [1. Middle East—Emigration and immigration.] I. Title. II. Series.
   E184.A65N66 2004
   304.8'73056—dc22
                                                                              2003018746

THE CHANGING Face of North America: IMMIGRATION SINCE 1965

CONTENTS

Introduction
Senator Edward M. Kennedy   6

Foreword
Marian L. Smith   8
Peter A. Hammerschmidt   11

A Mosaic of Diversity   15

Friends, Enemies, and Neighbors   23

Leaving the Homeland   37

Making a New Life   61

Fitting In   69

Stereotypes, Discrimination, and Other Problems   83

An Uncertain Future   97

Famous Middle Eastern Americans/Canadians   102

Glossary   103

Further Reading   104

Internet Resources   105

Index   106

INTRODUCTION

THE CHANGING FACE OF AMERICA

By Senator Edward M. Kennedy

America is proud of its heritage and history as a nation of immigrants, and my own family is an example. All eight of my great-grandparents were immigrants who left Ireland a century and a half ago, when that land was devastated by the massive famine caused by the potato blight. When I was a young boy, my grandfather used to take me down to the docks in Boston and regale me with stories about the Great Famine and the waves of Irish immigrants who came to America seeking a better life. He talked of how the Irish left their marks in Boston and across the nation, enduring many hardships and harsh discrimination, but also building the railroads, digging the canals, settling the West, and filling the factories of a growing America. According to one well-known saying of the time, "under every railroad tie, an Irishman is buried."

America was the promised land for them, as it has been for so many other immigrants who have found shelter, hope, opportunity, and freedom. Immigrants have always been an indispensable part of our nation. They have contributed immensely to our communities, created new jobs and whole new industries, served in our armed forces, and helped make America the continuing land of promise that it is today.

The inspiring poem by Emma Lazarus, inscribed on the pedestal of the Statue of Liberty in New York Harbor, is America's welcome to all immigrants:

Give me your tired, your poor,
Your huddled masses yearning to breathe free,
The wretched refuse of your teeming shore,
Send these, the homeless, tempest-tossed, to me:
I lift my lamp beside the golden door.

The period since September 11, 2001, has been particularly challenging for immigrants. Since the horrifying terrorist attacks, there has been a resurgence of anti-immigrant attitudes and behavior. We all agree that our borders must be safe and secure. Yet, at the same time, we must safeguard the entry of the millions of persons who come to the United States legally each year as immigrants, visitors, scholars, students, and workers. The "golden door" must stay open. We must recognize that immigration is not the problem—terrorism is. We must identify and isolate the terrorists, and not isolate America.

One of my most important responsibilities in the Senate is the preservation of basic rights and basic fairness in the application of our immigration laws, so that new generations of immigrants in our own time and for all time will have the same opportunity that my great-grandparents had when they arrived in America.

Immigration is beneficial for the United States and for countries throughout the world. It is no coincidence that two hundred years ago, our nations' founders chose *E Pluribus Unum*—"out of many, one"—as America's motto. These words, chosen by Benjamin Franklin, John Adams, and Thomas Jefferson, refer to the ideal that separate colonies can be transformed into one united nation. Today, this ideal has come to apply to individuals as well. Our diversity is our strength. We are a nation of immigrants, and we always will be.

FOREWORD

THE CHANGING FACE OF THE UNITED STATES

Marian L. Smith, historian
U.S. Immigration and Naturalization Service

Americans commonly assume that immigration today is very different than immigration of the past. The immigrants themselves appear to be unlike immigrants of earlier eras. Their language, their dress, their food, and their ways seem strange. At times people fear too many of these new immigrants will destroy the America they know. But has anything really changed? Do new immigrants have any different effect on America than old immigrants a century ago? Is the American fear of too much immigration a new development? Do immigrants really change America more than America changes the immigrants? The very subject of immigration raises many questions.

In the United States, immigration is more than a chapter in a history book. It is a continuous thread that links the present moment to the first settlers on North American shores. From the first colonists' arrival until today, immigrants have been met by Americans who both welcomed and feared them. Immigrant contributions were always welcome—on the farm, in the fields, and in the factories. Welcoming the poor, the persecuted, and the "huddled masses" became an American principle. Beginning with the original Pilgrims' flight from religious persecution in the 1600s, through the Irish migration to escape starvation in the 1800s, to the relocation of Central Americans seeking refuge from civil wars in the 1980s and 1990s, the United States has considered itself a haven for the destitute and the oppressed.

But there was also concern that immigrants would not adopt American ways, habits, or language. Too many immigrants might overwhelm America. If so, the dream of the Founding Fathers for United States government and society would be destroyed. For this reason, throughout American history some have argued that limiting or ending immigration is our patriotic duty. Benjamin Franklin feared there were so many German immigrants in Pennsylvania the Colonial Legislature would begin speaking German. "Progressive" leaders of the early 1900s feared that immigrants who could not read and understand the English language were not only exploited by "big business," but also served as the foundation for "machine politics" that undermined the U.S. Constitution. This theme continues today, usually voiced by those who bear no malice toward immigrants but who want to preserve American ideals.

Have immigrants changed? In colonial days, when most colonists were of English descent, they considered Germans, Swiss, and French immigrants as different. They were not "one of us" because they spoke a different language. Generations later, Americans of German or French descent viewed Polish, Italian, and Russian immigrants as strange. They were not "like us" because they had a different religion, or because they did not come from a tradition of constitutional government. Recently, Americans of Polish or Italian descent have seen Nicaraguan, Pakistani, or Vietnamese immigrants as too different to be included. It has long been said of American immigration that the latest ones to arrive usually want to close the door behind them.

It is important to remember that fear of individual immigrant groups seldom lasted, and always lessened. Benjamin Franklin's anxiety over German immigrants disappeared after those immigrants' sons and daughters helped the nation gain independence in the Revolutionary War. The Irish of the mid-1800s were among the most hated immigrants, but today we all wear green on St. Patrick's Day. While a century ago it was feared that Italian and other Catholic immigrants would vote as directed by the Pope, today that controversy is only a vague memory. Unfortunately, some ethnic groups continue their efforts to earn acceptance. The African

Americans' struggle continues, and some Asian Americans, whose families have been in America for generations, are the victims of current anti-immigrant sentiment.

Time changes both immigrants and America. Each wave of new immigrants, with their strange language and habits, eventually grows old and passes away. Their American-born children speak English. The immigrants' grandchildren are completely American. The strange foods of their ancestors—spaghetti, baklava, hummus, or tofu—become common in any American restaurant or grocery store. Much of what the immigrants brought to these shores is lost, principally their language. And what is gained becomes as American as St. Patrick's Day, Hanukkah, or Cinco de Mayo, and we forget that it was once something foreign.

Recent immigrants are all around us. They come from every corner of the earth to join in the American Dream. They will continue to help make the American Dream a reality, just as all the immigrants who came before them have done.

THE CHANGING FACE OF CANADA

Peter A. Hammerschmidt
First Secretary, Permanent Mission of Canada to the United Nations

Throughout Canada's history, immigration has shaped and defined the very character of Canadian society. The migration of peoples from every part of the world into Canada has profoundly changed the way we look, speak, eat, and live. Through close and distant relatives who left their lands in search of a better life, all Canadians have links to immigrant pasts. We are a nation built by and of immigrants.

Two parallel forces have shaped the history of Canadian immigration. The enormous diversity of Canada's immigrant population is the most obvious. In the beginning came the enterprising settlers of the "New World," the French and English colonists. Soon after came the Scottish, Irish, and Northern and Central European farmers of the 1700s and 1800s. As the country expanded westward during the mid-1800s, migrant workers began arriving from China, Japan, and other Asian countries. And the turbulent twentieth century brought an even greater variety of immigrants to Canada, from the Caribbean, Africa, India, and Southeast Asia.

So while English- and French-Canadians are the largest ethnic groups in the country today, neither group alone represents a majority of the population. A large and vibrant multicultural mix makes up the rest, particularly in Canada's major cities. Toronto, Vancouver, and Montreal alone are home to people from over 200 ethnic groups!

Less obvious but equally important in the evolution of Canadian immigration has been hope. The promise of a better life lured Europeans and Americans seeking cheap (sometimes even free) farmland. Thousands of Scots and Irish arrived to escape grinding poverty and starvation. Others came for freedom, to escape religious and political persecution. Canada has long been a haven to the world's dispossessed and disenfranchised—Dutch and German farmers cast out for their religious beliefs, black slaves fleeing the United States, and political refugees of despotic regimes in Europe, Africa, Asia, and South America.

The two forces of diversity and hope, so central to Canada's past, also shaped the modern era of Canadian immigration. Following the Second World War, Canada drew heavily on these influences to forge trailblazing immigration initiatives.

The catalyst for change was the adoption of the Canadian Bill of Rights in 1960. Recognizing its growing diversity and Canadians' changing attitudes towards racism, the government passed a federal statute barring discrimination on the grounds of race, national origin, color, religion, or sex. Effectively rejecting the discriminatory elements in Canadian immigration policy, the Bill of Rights forced the introduction of a new policy in 1962. The focus of immigration abruptly switched from national origin to the individual's potential contribution to Canadian society. The door to Canada was now open to every corner of the world.

Welcoming those seeking new hopes in a new land has also been a feature of Canadian immigration in the modern era. The focus on economic immigration has increased along with Canada's steadily growing economy, but political immigration has also been encouraged. Since 1945, Canada has admitted tens of thousands of displaced persons, including Jewish Holocaust survivors, victims of Soviet crackdowns in Hungary and Czechoslovakia, and refugees from political upheaval in Uganda, Chile, and Vietnam.

Prior to 1978, however, these political refugees were admitted as an exception to normal immigration procedures. That year, Canada revamped its refugee policy with a new Immigration Act that explicitly affirmed Canada's commitment to the resettlement of refugees from oppression. Today, the admission of refugees remains a central part of Canadian immigration law and regulations.

Amendments to economic and political immigration policy continued during the 1980s and 1990s, refining further the bold steps taken during the modern era. Together, these initiatives have turned Canada into one of the world's few truly multicultural states.

Unlike the process of assimilation into a "melting pot" of cultures, immigrants to Canada are more likely to retain their cultural identity, beliefs, and practices. This is the source of some of Canada's greatest strengths as a society. And as a truly multicultural nation, diversity is not seen as a threat to Canadian identity. Quite the contrary—diversity *is* Canadian identity.

1

A MOSAIC
OF DIVERSITY

Like a tile mosaic, the Middle East is one large, complex picture made up of many small and unique pieces. The presence of Arabs and non-Arabs; Muslims, Christians, and Jews; and Kurds, Berbers, and other ethnic groups adds shades of color to (and often overshadows) national affiliations. The distinctions sometimes blur. For example, some Arabs are Christians, and many Arab countries are also home to small Jewish communities. Iran and Turkey—among the most populous countries in the region—are not Arab at all. Kurds and Palestinians, two peoples without a homeland, are scattered throughout various Middle Eastern countries.

Not even the definition of the Middle East is set in stone. Some people use the term in a strictly geographic sense, to denote the countries of southwest Asia and northeastern Africa; for others, the Middle East is a political designation that also includes all the predominantly Muslim countries in North Africa. As used in this book, the term *Middle East* will include Algeria, Bahrain, Egypt, Iraq, Jordan, Kuwait, Lebanon, Libya, Morocco, Oman, Qatar, Saudi Arabia, Sudan, Syria, Tunisia, the United Arab Emirates, Yemen, and the Palestinians—all the members of the Arab League with the exception of Somalia, Mauritania, Djibouti, and Comoros, which are actually not Arab countries—as well as Iran, Israel, and Turkey.

◀ The Middle East comprises a multitude of peoples and cultures. The crowd in this 2001 photo has assembled in Jerusalem to demonstrate for peace between Palestinians and Israelis.

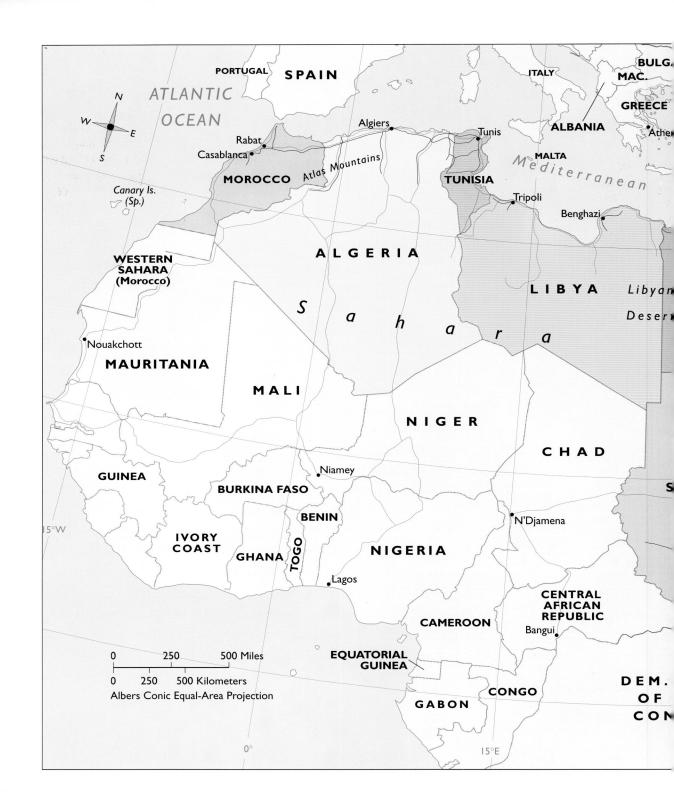

ATLANTIC
OCEAN

PORTUGAL   SPAIN

ITALY

BULG.

MAC.

GREECE

ALBANIA

Athen

N
W   E
S

Algiers

Rabat

Casablanca

Tunis

MALTA

Mediterranean

Canary Is.
(Sp.)

MOROCCO   Atlas Mountains

TUNISIA

Tripoli

Benghazi

WESTERN
SAHARA
(Morocco)

ALGERIA

LIBYA   Libyan

Deser

S   a   h   a   r   a

Nouakchott

MAURITANIA

MALI

NIGER

CHAD

GUINEA

Niamey

BURKINA FASO

N'Djamena

S

15°W

BENIN

IVORY
COAST

GHANA   TOGO

NIGERIA

Lagos

CENTRAL
AFRICAN
REPUBLIC

CAMEROON

Bangui

0   250   500 Miles

0   250   500 Kilometers

Albers Conic Equal-Area Projection

EQUATORIAL
GUINEA

CONGO

DEM.
OF
CON

GABON

0°   15°E

The Middle Eastern countries discussed in this book are shown in color on this map. Although definitions of what constitutes the Middle East differ, this book will include information about the major Arab states of the Arabian Peninsula and North Africa, as well as Israel, Turkey, and Iran.

Key

——	Railroad
——	Road
++++	Canal

Given the ethnic and cultural diversity of these countries, it should come as no surprise that there is no "typical" Middle Eastern American or Canadian. The Arab American community, in particular, has diversified. In *Arabs in America: Building a New Future*, author Lisa Suhair Majaj observes:

> In contrast to the earlier Arab immigrant population, composed largely of Christians from Mount Lebanon, the current Arab-American community is far from homogenous. It includes people of many different national origins and religions; recent immigrants and assimilated descendants of earlier immigrants; dark-skinned and light-skinned individuals; people who speak no Arabic, those who speak no English, and those whose dialects are unintelligible to each other; and children of mixed marriages whose hybrid identities locate them at the margins of "Arab" and "American" identity.

Middle Easterners have lived in North America since the late 1800s. But changes in immigration policy have increased the numbers of Middle Eastern people able to enter the United States or Canada. In the United States, the landmark legislation was the Immigration Act of 1965, which removed "national origin" quotas that severely limited the number of Middle Easterners, Asians, certain southern Europeans, and other ethnic groups who could immigrate to the United States. Similarly, a reformed immigration policy in Canada, instituted in 1967, enabled more people from underrepresented ethnic groups to live in that country.

The 1965 U.S. law not only brought more Middle Eastern immigrants to the United States, it invited a more diverse mix. In an essay she contributed to *Arabs in America: Building a New Future*," Helen Hatab Samhan, executive director of the Arab American Institute Foundation, notes:

> In the past 30 years, not only did new Arab immigration diversify and expand the Arab American community, it also brought about political, cultural, and religious identities that contrasted with the assimilated identity of the U.S.-born co-ethnics. Where offspring of the first (mostly Christian) immigrants had faced the intensive civic assimilation of that largely European wave, the post–World War II immigrants arrived in a wave predominantly from the Third World, a factor that would also characterize their identity and attitudes toward assimilation in general and classification in particular.

In recent decades, the number of Middle Eastern immigrants living in the United States has grown dramatically—from fewer than 200,000 in 1970 to approximately 1.5 million by the beginning of the 21st century. A large proportion of these people have settled in New York, California, Michigan, New Jersey, and Virginia.

The number of Middle Eastern immigrants to the United States has swelled from fewer than 200,000 in 1970 to about 1.5 million at the beginning of the 21st century. Some countries, such as Oman and Bahrain, have contributed only a few hundred to this total; by contrast, hundreds of thousands of immigrants have come from Iran. In Canada, Iran is the leading source of immigrants among Middle Eastern countries. (Most figures presented here are from the U.S. Bureau of Citizenship and Immigration Services—formerly the Immigration and Naturalization Service—and from Citizenship and Immigration Canada. Complete figures are not available for all years from all Middle Eastern countries, but those that are published show generally increasing immigration to the United States and Canada from most of the Middle East.)

These numbers reflect only new immigrants, however. By heritage, the Middle Eastern community in North America is much larger, with about 3 million to 4 million people of Arab descent (both Christian and Muslim) and about 5 million Jews (although most North American Jews trace their family's heritage to Europe, not the Middle East).

And yet, counting some Middle Eastern Americans—Arab Americans specifically—becomes a more difficult issue. As of 2000, the U.S. Census Bureau did not include an Arab America category. In her poem "Browner Shades of White," Laila Halal observes, "I am white, because there is no square for exotic." Without an Arab American category recognized by the U.S. government, the remaining tool for tracking Middle Eastern ethnicity on the census (although an imperfect one) is the question on ancestry. The question appears only on the long form of the census, which is given to about 17 percent of the population.

A New Country, A New Life

Najat Mounir's outlook has been shaped by what she describes as "the unusual aspect of the path my life took, and all the extraordinary events that took place during the journey." Mounir's journey began in Casablanca, where she was the 5th of 10 children born to a poor Moroccan couple. At 16, she was wed to an illiterate man three times her age—an arranged marriage that lasted about a year. Mounir went to college in France but soon became pregnant and dropped out of school.

Back in Morocco, she took a job at an airport, but she began dreaming of a fresh start in the United States. She eventually immigrated, settling first in New York City, then in Las Vegas, and finally in a small town in Washington. Mounir's dream has not always been easy. She's been separated from her first son, who lives in Morocco, for many years; she's gone through bankruptcy; and she now raises a second son as a single mother. But she has also experienced a great deal of joy in her adopted country.

In her essay "Awareness! What Does It Take?" Mounir writes, "I shared joy, pain, and dreams with people of all nations here in America, and found out, we are all the same. Here I am treated as a human being in my community. . . . I am not a case file, a statistic, or a number. I am not looked upon as a stranger, a foreigner, or a terrorist either. Instead of the image of a stranger Arab Muslim woman, people here know me as the Arab Muslim woman who is Zacharia's mom."

They're Still Coming to America

The reasons Middle Easterners leave their homelands, and how they fare once they arrive in North America, will be explored in later chapters. Although poverty does exist among Middle Eastern immigrants, generally speaking, they are better educated, earn more money, and become American citizens in higher percentages than immigrants from many other parts of the world. That's not to say that Middle Eastern immigrants do not have barriers and obstacles to overcome; in that, they are similar to other newcomers.

The motivating factors that brought Middle Easterners to North America continued for many years after immigration quotas were lifted in the 1960s. Then, beginning on September 11, 2001, the course of Middle Eastern immigration became unclear. On that day, terrorist hijackers crashed airplanes into both towers of New York's World Trade Center and into the Pentagon, outside Washington, D.C.; another plane, believed to be headed for the White House or U.S. Capitol, crashed in a field in western Pennsylvania. In all, about 3,000 people were killed in the attacks.

The 19 terrorists were associates of al-Qaeda, the Islamic militant organization led by Osama bin Laden. Bin Laden's desire to overthrow governments he considered to be "non-Islamic" and to rid Muslim countries of non-Muslims was well known, but never before had such an attack been launched on American soil.

The hijackers were all from Middle Eastern countries, primarily Saudi Arabia. They had entered the United States legally on temporary visas as students, tourists, or businessmen, and at the time of the attack, 16 of the 19 were still in the country legally. When this fact later emerged, it stirred much debate about the U.S. immigration system.

However, despite an escalation in anti-Arab sentiment following the September 11 attacks, many analysts expect immigration to the United States by Middle Easterners to grow.

2 FRIENDS, ENEMIES, AND NEIGHBORS

To understand the modern Middle East, and to get a sense of why people from the region emigrate, a little historical background is helpful. The Middle East is considered a cradle of civilization. Agriculture developed in Mesopotamia, the region between the Tigris and Euphrates Rivers in present-day Iraq, around 8000 B.C. By the fourth millennium B.C. the world's first cities had sprung up in southern Mesopotamia under the Sumerians; the Sumerians also created the earliest-known system of writing.

Over the centuries the Middle East gave rise to a number of important kingdoms and empires, including ancient Egypt, Babylonia, and Assyria. Located at a strategically important crossroads between the Mediterranean world and the Far East, the region also attracted many foreign conquerors, including Alexander the Great in the fourth century B.C.

The Roman Empire at its height controlled much of the Middle East, including Asia Minor (modern-day Turkey), Mesopotamia, the eastern shores of the Mediterranean (territory that today includes Syria, Lebanon, and Israel), Egypt, and a long swath of land running along the coast of North Africa from Egypt to present-day Morocco. As far as the Middle East is concerned, however, Rome's most enduring legacy may be its treatment of one of the peoples under its dominion: the Jews.

A people unified by their monotheistic religion—and specifically by the belief that God had established a covenant with

◀ Constructed in the mid-14th century A.D., the Sultan Hassan Mosque in Cairo, Egypt, is an outstanding example of Islamic architecture. Islam dominates the contemporary Middle East and North Africa, where more than 9 in 10 people are Muslims.

them as His chosen people—the Jews had established a powerful kingdom, with its spiritual and political capital at Jerusalem, by around the 11th century B.C. Over the ensuing centuries, parts or all of the Jewish land fell to a succession of conquerors, including the Assyrians, the Babylonians, and the Macedonians under Alexander the Great.

In 63 B.C. Rome took control of Judea, as the Jews' land was called. But the Romans permitted the Jews a degree of autonomy. However, the Romans clamped down hard on a Jewish revolt that began in A.D. 66. In 70, after four years of fighting, the Romans sacked Jerusalem and destroyed the Jews' Holy Temple. After suppressing another revolt, the Bar Kochba Rebellion, in 165, the Romans forbade Jews to enter Jerusalem, exiled the majority of the Jewish population, and renamed the area Palestine (after the Jews' traditional enemies, the Philistines).

By this time another major monotheistic faith, Christianity, had sprung up in the region. That religion centered on Jesus of Nazareth, a Jew whom the Romans executed around A.D. 30.

European Christian knights under Godfrey of Bouillon celebrate the taking of Jerusalem from the Muslims during the First Crusade, July 15, 1099. Possession of the city of Jerusalem—holy ground for all three of the major monotheistic religions that originated in the Middle East—has been a source of conflict for centuries.

Followers came to believe that Jesus was the Son of God and that his death redeemed sinful humanity. The Romans initially persecuted Christians, but in the early fourth century the Roman emperor Constantine converted to the new faith, and by the end of the century Christianity had become the empire's official state religion. This greatly facilitated Christianity's spread.

The Rise of Islam

Beginning in the seventh century, the Middle East came under the influence of the third major monotheistic religion to arise in the region: Islam. The faithful believe that around 610 Muhammad, an Arab merchant living in Mecca (in present-day Saudi Arabia), received the first of a lifelong series of revelations from Allah (God). Soon thereafter Muhammad began preaching Allah's message—the essence of which is that there is only one God and that believers must submit to God's will. Forced to leave Mecca in 622, Muhammad and his followers settled in Medina. For the remainder of the decade, the Muslims (as adherents of Islam are called) fought the pagan Meccans, eventually triumphing and converting their enemies to the Islamic faith.

Soon after Muhammad's death in 632, a formidable Arab army emerged from the Arabian Peninsula and began a remarkable series of conquests that, in a matter of decades, would spread Islam's influence across the Middle East and North Africa and, by the early part of the eighth century, into Spain.

Yet the Islamic world was never completely united. Over the years, rival dynasties struggled for political control as various Islamic empires rose and fell. And religious differences among the faithful also emerged. A major doctrinal rift, which dates to Islam's earliest days, stemmed from the question of who should succeed Muhammad as caliph, or leader of Islam. One group, which came to be called the Sunni, believed that the caliph should be elected from among the Prophet's followers. Another group, known as the Shia, insisted that only a blood relative of Muhammad could serve as caliph. The split became quite bitter. Today, most Muslims worldwide follow the Sunni branch of Islam, though in a few Middle Eastern countries—notably Iran and Iraq—Shiites constitute a majority.

If Islam has suffered its share of internal conflicts, over the centuries relations among Muslims, Christians, and Jews have also frequently been troubled. This is the case despite the fact that the three faiths share many important connections. Christianity, of course, developed from Judaism; the two faiths diverged with the figure of Jesus, whom Christians believe to be the Messiah that God promised the Jewish people. But Islam, too, shares much with the Jewish tradition. Like Jews, Muslims trace their ancestry to the patriarch Abraham. Islam's prophets include Abraham, as well as Moses and Jesus. And for adherents of all three religions, the city of Jerusalem has special religious significance: for Jews, it is the site where the Holy Temple once stood; for Christians, it's where Jesus taught and was crucified; for Muslims, it's where the prophet Muhammad ascended to heaven. Much blood has been shed over control of Jerusalem, from the Crusades of the Middle Ages, during which European Christian knights fought to drive out the Muslims (and also massacred many Jews), to the present-day Palestinian-Israeli conflict.

The Ottoman Era

During the 16th century, the powerful Ottoman Empire began to extend its influence throughout the Middle East and North Africa. Though Muslims, the Ottomans—who also conquered southeastern Europe and the strategic area between the Black and Caspian Seas—were ethnic Turks rather than Arabs.

From their capital of Istanbul, in modern-day Turkey, the Ottomans administered their large empire through local governors. They were fairly liberal, allowing freedom of religion and limited self-rule among conquered peoples. Nevertheless, many Arabs deeply resented the idea of being under the authority of

Istanbul was the seat of Ottoman power from the mid-15th to the early 20th century. Today the Turkish city is a popular tourist destination, offering such attractions as the Blue Mosque.

the Ottoman sultan, not to mention the taxes they were compelled to pay to the empire.

In the opinion of most historians, the Ottoman Empire reached its peak during the reign of Süleyman the Magnificent (1520–1566). Over the next 350 years, corruption would weaken the empire from within, while the rise of European powers such as Russia, France, and Great Britain would pressure it from without. By 1914 the Ottoman Empire still held Mesopotamia, Palestine, and the Hejaz (the western part of present-day Saudi Arabia), but European colonial powers controlled, through various arrangements, much of North Africa, including Algeria, Morocco, and Tunisia (France); Egypt and the Sudan (Britain); and Libya (Italy).

World War I and Its Aftermath

When World War I broke out in 1914, the Ottoman Empire aligned itself with Germany and Austria-Hungary against the

Allies—principally Great Britain, France, and Russia. (The United States entered the war on the side of the Allies three years later.)

Following a disastrous campaign on Turkey's Gallipoli Peninsula in 1915, the British attempted to strike a blow against the Ottoman Turks by fomenting an Arab rebellion against them. In return for his support, the British promised the leader of that rebellion, Sharif Hussein bin Ali, that an Arab state would be created from Ottoman territory after the war. The exact boundaries of that state were never specified.

In 1917 the British also attempted to shore up Jewish support for the war effort by promising to "view with favour the establishment in Palestine of a national home for the Jewish people." Although the document in which this promise was made, the Balfour Declaration, explicitly stated that "nothing shall be done which may prejudice the civil and religious rights of existing non-Jewish communities in Palestine," Jews and Arabs

By the outbreak of World War I in 1914, European powers had whittled away much of the Ottoman Empire. After the war, League of Nations mandates gave administrative control of the remainder (except Turkey) to Great Britain and France.

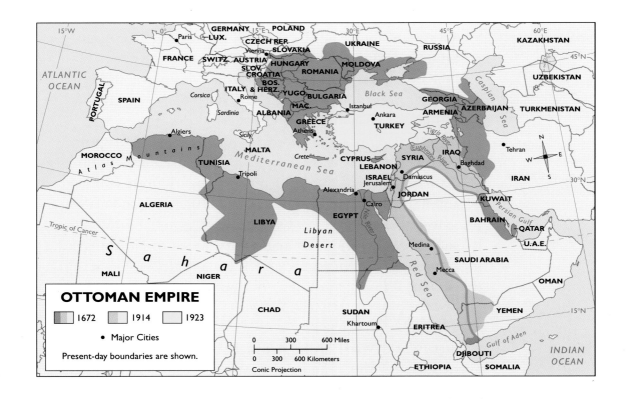

OTTOMAN EMPIRE

1672   1914   1923

• Major Cities

Present-day boundaries are shown.

0   300   600 Miles
0   300   600 Kilometers
Conic Projection

would prove unable to share the land peacefully.

In the meantime, however, the British had concluded a secret agreement with the French regarding the shape of the postwar Middle East. By the terms of the 1916 Sykes-Picot accord, the two countries agreed to divide the Ottoman territories of the region between themselves. The specifics of the agreement would be rendered obsolete by events on the ground, as Britain succeeded in conquering Palestine and Mesopotamia.

After the end of World War I in 1918, the defeated Ottoman Turks were forced to give up the remnants of their Middle Eastern empire (the modern Republic of Turkey emerged in 1923). The newly created League of Nations granted Great Britain and France mandates to administer Arab territories formerly under the control of the Ottoman Turks. Britain received the mandate for Mesopotamia (Iraq) and Palestine (which it later divided into Palestine and the Transjordan); France was awarded the mandate for Syria (including Lebanon) and the Hejaz.

The seeds of several intractable problems were sown during the post–World War I era. For example, the Kurds, a non-Arab people who occupy mountainous regions in modern-day Turkey, Iraq, Iran, and Syria, were supposed to be given a homeland, according to the terms of the Treaty of Sèvres. That did not happen, and Kurdish nationalism, particularly in Turkey, has led to bloodshed and remains a concern of the Turkish government. The kingdom of Iraq, which achieved independence in 1932 under a British-installed monarch born in Mecca, incorporated three distinct groups with separate national interests: ethnic Kurds, Sunni Muslims, and Shia Muslims. In the aftermath of the 2003 war that ousted Iraq's longtime dictator, Saddam Hussein, many analysts wondered whether Iraq would fracture along these lines. And in Palestine, Zionism—the movement to create a Jewish state—sparked violence between Jewish settlers and Palestinian Arabs. In the early years of the 21st century, the Jewish-Palestinian conflict remains at the heart of Middle East violence and instability.

Post–World War II Developments

During the period between World War II (1939–1945) and the 1960s, nation after nation in the Middle East and North Africa gained independence. In many cases, peace and stability have proved more elusive. Israel, for example, fought wars against its Arab neighbors at its founding in 1948, in 1967, and again in 1973; terrorism against Israel, particularly by Palestinians who want to establish their own homeland, has occurred continually since the 1960s. Iraq invaded its neighbors Iran in 1980 and Kuwait in 1990. The former invasion led to an extremely costly eight-year stalemate; the latter, to defeat

Birthplace of Religions

The Middle East has given birth to the world's three most important monotheistic religions: Judaism, Christianity, and Islam.

Today, more than 90 percent of Middle Easterners and North Africans are followers of Islam. Yet none of the four largest Muslim nations (Indonesia, Pakistan, India, and Bangladesh) are located in the Middle East. Like other religions, Islam can be interpreted in different ways. Nonetheless, there are five basic beliefs, or pillars, that define the religion: faith, specifically that there is only one God and that Muhammad was his last and greatest prophet; prayers, said five times daily; charity to provide for the needy; fasting; and pilgrimage to the holy city of Mecca. Most Middle Eastern Muslims are either Sunni or Shiite, two branches of Islam that developed over the question of who was Muhammad's rightful successor. In the Middle East, most Shiites live in Iran, Iraq, or southern Lebanon.

Middle Eastern Christians are relatively few in number and, in some cases, persecuted or limited in their ability to practice their faith. They believe in a three-person God, or Holy Trinity (Father, Son, and Holy Spirit), and believe that the Son, Jesus, was crucified and resurrected, in the process redeeming humanity. Most Middle Eastern Christians are members of Eastern Rite churches (Armenian, Chaldean, Coptic, Maronite, Melkite, and Syrian), which are affiliated with the Roman Catholic Church. However, Eastern Rite churches are semi-autonomous, meaning they observe the core beliefs of the Catholic Church as well as their own customs and rites. For example, Eastern Rite clergy are permitted to marry, while Roman Catholic priests are not.

at the hands of a U.S.-led coalition in 1991. Lebanon suffered through a civil war that lasted from 1975 to 1990 and claimed more than 140,000 lives. Sudan's civil war was even more pitiless, leading to an estimated 2 million deaths between 1983 and 2001. Algeria has seen long-running violence between Arabs and Berbers, and between those who support fundamentalist Islamic rule and those who favor a moderate, secular government.

In the political realm, the Middle East is remarkable for its dearth of fully democratic, representative governments—with the notable exceptions of Israel and Turkey. That is not to say

(continued on p. 35)

Not all Eastern Rite churches share the same beliefs or operate in the same region. For instance, the Maronites, unlike other Christians, believe that Jesus Christ was fully divine, and not also human. Most Maronites live in Lebanon, composing about one-fourth of the country's population. While there are more than 4 million Coptic Christians living in Egypt, they are discriminated against and often severely persecuted. Many Middle Eastern Chaldean Christians live in Iraq, where they account for about 3 percent of the population; even today, they speak Aramaic, the language Jesus is believed to have spoken. Pockets of Christian communities can also be found in Jordan, Israel, and Iran, but Christianity is against the law in Saudi Arabia.

More than 6 million people live in Israel, and about 5 million of them are Jews. According to Jewish teaching, Jews are God's chosen people and are awaiting a Messiah, a deliverer. In 1948, following World War II, the State of Israel was established. Among the many Jews who immigrated to Israel during that period were Jewish survivors of the Holocaust in Europe and Jews living in Arab countries.

The Druze, members of a secretive sect that originated about a thousand years ago as an offshoot of Islam, believe their religion to be a reinterpretation of Islam, Christianity, and Judaism. But they do not observe religious rituals or accept converts; they do believe in reincarnation. Most of the estimated 1 million Druze today live in Syria, Lebanon, or Israel. In Israel, the Druze have their own legal and educational systems.

Middle East Nations at a Glance

Algeria

Area: 918,497 sq. miles
Capital: Algiers
Independence: July 5, 1962 (from France)
Population: 32,818,500
Ethnic groups: Arab-Berber, 99%; European, less than 1%
GDP per capita: $5,300

Bahrain

Area: 255 sq. miles
Capital: Manama
Independence: August 15, 1971 (from Great Britain)
Population: 667,238 (includes 235,108 non-nationals)
Ethnic groups: Bahraini, 63%; Asian, 19%; other Arab, 10%; Iranian, 8%
GDP per capita: $14,000

Egypt

Area: 386,900 sq. miles
Capital: Cairo
Independence: February 28, 1922 (from Great Britain)
Population: 74,718,797
Ethnic groups: Eastern Hamitic stock (Egyptians, Bedouins, and Berbers), 99%; Greek, Nubian, Armenian, other European (primarily Italian and French), 1%
GDP per capita: $3,900

Iran

Area: 635,932 sq. miles
Capital: Tehran
Independence: April 1, 1979 (proclamation of the Islamic Republic of Iran)
Population: 68,278,826
Ethnic groups: Persian, 51%; Azeri, 24%; Gilaki and Mazandarani, 8%; Kurd, 7%; Arab, 3%; Lur, 2%; Baloch, 2%; Turkmen, 2%; other, 1%
GDP per capita: $7,000

Iraq

Area: 168,927 sq. miles
Capital: Baghdad
Independence: October 3, 1932 (from British administration under League of Nations mandate)
Population: 24,683,313
Ethnic groups: Arab, 75%–80%; Kurdish, 15%–20%; Turkoman, Assyrian, or other, 5%
GDP per capita: $2,400

Israel

Area: 7,992 sq. miles
Capital: Jerusalem
Independence: May 14, 1948 (from British administration under League of Nations mandate)
Population: 6,116,533 (July 2002 est.) (Note: includes about 390,000 Israeli settlers in occupied areas of West Bank, East Jerusalem, Gaza Strip, and Golan Heights)
Ethnic groups: Jewish, 80.1%; non-Jewish (mostly Arab), 19.9% (1996 est.)
GDP per capita: $19,000

Jordan

Area: 34,575 sq. miles
Capital: Amman
Independence: May 25, 1946 (from British administration under League of Nations mandate)
Population: 5,460,265
Ethnic groups: Arab, 98%; Circassian, 1%; Armenian, 1%
GDP per capita: $4,300

Kuwait

Area: 6,880 sq. miles
Capital: Kuwait
Independence: June 19, 1961 (from Great Britain)
Population: 2,183,161 (includes 1,291,354 non-nationals)

Ethnic groups: Kuwaiti, 45%; other Arab, 35%; South Asian, 9%; Iranian, 4%; other, 7%
GDP per capita: $15,000

Lebanon

Area: 3,949 sq. miles
Capital: Beirut
Independence: November 22, 1943 (from French administration under League of Nations mandate)
Population: 3,727,703
Ethnic groups: Arab, 95%; Armenian, 4%; other, 1%
GDP per capita: $5,400

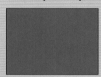

Libya

Area: 679,358 sq. miles
Capital: Tripoli
Independence: December 24, 1951 (from Italy)
Population: 5,499,074 (includes 166,510 non-nationals)
Ethnic groups: Berber and Arab, 97%; Greeks, Maltese, Italians, Egyptians, Pakistanis, Turks, Indians, Tunisians, 3%
GDP per capita: $7,600

Morocco

Area: 172,413 sq. miles
Capital: Rabat
Independence: March 2, 1956 (from France)
Population: 31,689,265
Ethnic groups: Arab-Berber, 99.1%; Jewish, 0.2%; other, 0.7%
GDP per capita: $3,900

Oman

Area: 82,000 sq. miles
Capital: Muscat
Independence: 1650 (expulsion of the Portuguese)
Population: 2,807,125 (includes 577,293 non-nationals)

Ethnic groups: Arab, Baluchi, South Asian (Indian, Pakistani, Sri Lankan, Bangladeshi), African
GDP per capita: $8,300

Qatar

Area: 4,400 sq. miles
Capital: Doha
Independence: September 3, 1971 (from Great Britain)
Population: 817,052
Ethnic groups: Arab, 40%; Pakistani, 18%; Indian, 18%; Iranian, 10%; other, 14%
GDP per capita: $21,500

Saudi Arabia

Area: about 865,000 sq. miles
Capital: Riyadh
Independence: September 23, 1932 (unification of the kingdom)
Population: 24,293,844 (includes 5,576,076 non-nationals)
Ethnic groups: Arab, 90%; Afro-Asian, 10%
GDP per capita: $10,500

Sudan

Area: 967,500 sq. miles
Capital: Khartoum
Independence: January 1, 1956 (from Egypt and Great Britain)
Population: 38,114,160
Ethnic groups: black, 52%; Arab, 39%; Beja, 6%; other, 3%
GDP per capita: $1,420

Syria

Area: 71,498 sq. miles
Capital: Damascus
Independence: April 17, 1946 (from French administration under League of Nations mandate)
Population: 17,585,540 (July 2002 est.) (Note: About 40,000 more people live in

Middle East Nations at a Glance

the Israeli-occupied Golan Heights.)
Ethnic groups: Arab, 90.3%; Kurds,
Armenians, and other, 9.7%
GDP per capita: $3,500

Tunisia

Area: 63,378 sq. miles
Capital: Tunis
Independence: March
20, 1956 (from France)
Population: 9,924,742
Ethnic groups: Arab, 98%; European, 1%;
Jewish and other, 1%
GDP per capita: $6,500

Turkey

Area: 301,380 sq. miles
Capital: Ankara
Independence: October
29, 1923 (successor
state to the Ottoman Empire)
Population: 68,109,469
Ethnic groups: Turkish, 80%; Kurdish,
20%
GDP per capita: $7,000

United Arab Emirates

Area: 31,992 sq. miles
Capital: Abu Dhabi
Independence:
December 2, 1971 (from Great Britain)
Population: 2,484,818 (includes an esti-
mated 1,606,079 non-nationals)
Ethnic groups: Emirati, 19%; other Arab
and Iranian, 23%; South Asian, 50%;
other expatriates (includes Westerners
and East Asians), 8% (1982)
(Note: As of 1982, less than 20% of the
population were UAE citizens.)
GDP per capita: $22,000

West Bank and Gaza Strip*

West Bank:
Area: 2,262 sq. miles
Population: 2,237,194 (July 2002 est.)
(Note: Population does not include an

estimated 364,000 Israeli settlers living in
the West Bank and East Jerusalem.)
Ethnic groups: Palestinian Arab and other,
83%; Jewish, 17%
GDP per capita: $800

Gaza Strip:
Area: 139 sq. miles
Population: 1,274,868 (July 2002 est.)
(Note: Population does not include about
5,000 Israeli settlers living in Gaza.)
Ethnic groups: Palestinian Arab and other,
99.4%; Jewish, 0.6%
GDP per capita: $600

Yemen

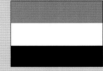

Area: 203,849 sq. miles
Capital: Sanaa
Independence:
Republic of Yemen
established May 22, 1990, with the
merger of North Yemen and South Yemen
Population: 19,349,881
Ethnic groups: predominantly Arab; but
also Afro-Arabs, South Asians, Europeans
GDP per capita: $840

*As of late 2003, the West Bank and Gaza Strip
remained under Israeli military occupation, although
the Palestinian Authority exercised limited control, in
keeping with earlier Israel-Palestinian agreements;
negotiations to determine the final status of the
territories had been suspended because of
continuing violence.

Notes: Unless otherwise indicated, population figures
are July 2003 estimates. All GDP per capita figures
are 2002 estimates.

Sources: CIA World Factbook, 2003;
Merriam-Webster's Geographical Dictionary, 3rd ed.

Palestinians in the West Bank town of Hebron stand next to the remains of a house demolished by the Israel Defense Forces in retaliation for the killing of two Israeli soldiers, December 2002. A solution to the decades-long Israeli-Palestinian conflict remains elusive.

that all the governments of the region are dictatorships like Libya under Colonel Muammar al-Qaddafi. For example, Egypt, Iran, and Algeria are, in theory, republics. But in Egypt all political parties must be approved by the government, and there is only one candidate in presidential elections; in Algeria the military has prevented free elections, fearing popular support for Islamic fundamentalists; and in Iran, which has an elected legislature and president, conservative Shiite clerics hold actual power. Monarchs rule, with greater or lesser degrees of authoritarianism, in Saudi Arabia, Kuwait, Jordan, and Morocco, among other Middle Eastern nations. Overall, exclusion from the political process is seen as a major factor in public unrest in the region.

3 LEAVING THE HOMELAND

People from the Middle East have been immigrating to North America for more than a century. Over that period, several significant changes have occurred in U.S. and Canadian immigration policy. In addition, North Americans' attitudes toward newcomers have varied.

A Brief History of U.S. Immigration to 1965

Immigration to the United States has been characterized by openness punctuated by periods of restriction. During the 17th, 18th, and 19th centuries, immigration was essentially open without restriction, and, at times, immigrants were even recruited to come to America. Between 1783 and 1820, approximately 250,000 immigrants arrived at U.S. shores. Between 1841 and 1860, more than 4 million immigrants came; most were from England, Ireland, and Germany.

Historically, race and ethnicity have played a role in legislation to restrict immigration. The Chinese Exclusion Act of 1882, which was not repealed until 1943, specifically prevented Chinese people from becoming U.S. citizens and did not allow Chinese laborers to immigrate for the next decade. An agreement with Japan in the early 1900s prevented most Japanese immigration to the United States.

Until the 1920s, no numerical restrictions on immigration existed in the United States, although health restrictions

◄The Registry Hall on Ellis Island, circa 1905. Between 1892 and 1954, about 12 million immigrants to the United States passed through this famous immigration station in New York Harbor.

applied. The only other significant restrictions came in 1917, when passing a literacy test became a requirement for immigrants. Presidents Cleveland, Taft, and Wilson had vetoed similar measures earlier. In addition, in 1917 a prohibition was added to the law against the immigration of people from Asia (defined as the Asiatic barred zone). While a few of these prohibitions were lifted during World War II, they were not repealed until 1952, and even then Asians were allowed in only under very small annual quotas.

During World War I, the federal government required that all travelers to the United States obtain a visa at a U.S. consulate or diplomatic post abroad. As former State Department consular affairs officer C. D. Scully points out, by making that requirement permanent Congress, by 1924, established the framework of temporary, or non-immigrant visas (for study, work, or travel), and immigrant visas (for permanent residence). That framework remains in place today.

Immigrants have not always been welcomed into the United States. This cartoon, published in 1881 in the San Francisco–based magazine the *Wasp*, attributes a host of social ills, including immorality, disease, filth, and the ruin of "white labor," to Chinese immigrants. The following year, Congress passed the Chinese Exclusion Act of 1882.

After World War I, cultural intolerance and bizarre racial theories led to new immigration restrictions. The House Judiciary Committee employed a eugenics consultant, Dr. Harry N. Laughlin, who asserted that certain races were inferior. Another leader of the eugenics movement, Madison Grant, argued that Jews, Italians, and others were inferior because of their supposedly different skull size.

The Immigration Act of 1924, preceded by the Temporary Quota Act of 1921, set new numerical limits on immigration based on "national origin." Taking effect in 1929, the 1924 act set annual quotas on immigrants that were specifically designed to keep out southern Europeans, such as Italians and Greeks. Generally no more than 100 people of the proscribed nationalities were permitted to immigrate.

While the new law was rigid, the U.S. Department of State's restrictive interpretation directed consular officers overseas to be even stricter in their application of the "public charge" provision. (A public charge is someone unable to support himself or his family.) According to author Laura Fermi, "In response to the new cry for restriction at the beginning of the [Great Depression] . . . the consuls were to interpret very strictly the clause prohibiting admission of aliens 'likely to become public charges; and to deny the visa to an applicant who in their opinion might become a public charge at any time.'"

In the early 1900s, more than one million immigrants a year came to the United States. In 1930—the first year of the national-origin quotas—approximately 241,700 immigrants were admitted. But under the State Department's strict interpretations, only 23,068 immigrants entered during 1933, the smallest total since 1831. Later these restrictions prevented many Jews in Germany and elsewhere in Europe from escaping what would become the Holocaust. At the height of the Holocaust in 1943, the United States admitted fewer than 6,000 refugees.

The Displaced Persons Act of 1948, the nation's first refugee law, allowed many refugees from World War II to settle in the

United States. The law put into place policy changes that had already seen immigration rise from 38,119 in 1945 to 108,721 in 1946 (and later to 249,187 in 1950). One-third of those admitted between 1948 and 1951 were Poles, with ethnic Germans forming the second-largest group.

The 1952 Immigration and Nationality Act is best known for its restrictions against those who supported communism or anarchy. However, the bill's other provisions were quite restrictive and were passed over the veto of President Truman. The 1952 act retained the national-origin quota system for the Eastern Hemisphere. The Western Hemisphere continued to operate without a quota and relied on other qualitative factors to limit immigration. Moreover, during that time, the Mexican bracero program, from 1942 to 1964, allowed millions of Mexican agricultural laborers to work temporarily in the United States.

The 1952 act set aside half of each national quota to be divided among three preference categories for relatives of U.S. citizens and permanent residents. The other half went to aliens with high education or exceptional abilities. These quotas applied only to those from the Eastern Hemisphere.

An End to the National-Origin Quotas

The Immigration and Nationality Act of 1965 became a landmark in immigration legislation by specifically striking the racially based national-origin quotas. It removed the barriers to Asian immigration, which later led to opportunities to immigrate for many Filipinos, Chinese, Koreans, and others. The Western Hemisphere was designated a ceiling of 120,000 immigrants but without a preference system or per country limits. Modifications made in 1978 ultimately combined the Western and Eastern Hemispheres into one preference system and one ceiling of 290,000.

The 1965 act built on the existing system—without the national-origin quotas—and gave somewhat more priority to family relationships. It did not completely overturn the existing

President Lyndon B. Johnson signed into law the Immigration Act of 1965, a milestone in U.S. immigration policy. The act eliminated the national-origin quota system that had been in place since the 1920s.

system but rather carried forward essentially intact the family immigration categories from the 1959 amendments to the Immigration and Nationality Act. Even though the text of the law prior to 1965 indicated that half of the immigration slots were reserved for skilled employment immigration, in practice, Immigration and Naturalization Service (INS) statistics show that 86 percent of the visas issued between 1952 and 1965 went for family immigration.

Developments Since 1980

A number of significant pieces of legislation since 1980 have shaped the current U.S. immigration system. First, the Refugee Act of 1980 removed refugees from the annual world limit and established that the president would set the number of refugees who could be admitted each year after consultations with Congress.

Second, the 1986 Immigration Reform and Control Act (IRCA) introduced sanctions against employers who "knowingly" hired undocumented immigrants (those in the country illegally). It also provided amnesty for many undocumented immigrants.

Third, the Immigration Act of 1990 increased legal immigration by 40 percent. In particular, the act significantly increased the number of employment-based immigrants (to 140,000), while also boosting family immigration.

Fourth, the 1996 Illegal Immigration Reform and Immigrant Responsibility Act (IIRAIRA) significantly tightened rules that permitted undocumented immigrants to convert to legal status and made other changes that tightened immigration law in areas such as political asylum and deportation.

Fifth, in response to the September 11, 2001, terrorist attacks, the USA PATRIOT Act and the Enhanced Border Security and Visa Entry Reform Act tightened rules on the granting of visas to individuals from certain countries and

As members of Congress look on, President George W. Bush signs the Enhanced Border Security and Visa Entry Reform Act, May 14, 2002.

enhanced the federal government's monitoring and detention authority over foreign nationals in the United States.

In a dramatic reorganization of the federal government, the Homeland Security Act of 2002 abolished the Immigration and Naturalization Service and transferred its immigration service and enforcement functions from the Department of Justice into a new Department of Homeland Security. The Customs Service, the Coast Guard, and parts of other agencies were also transferred into the new department.

The Department of Homeland Security, with regard to immigration, is organized as follows: The Bureau of Customs and Border Protection (BCBP) contains Customs and Immigration inspectors, who check the documents of travelers to the United States at air, sea, and land ports of entry; and Border Patrol agents, the uniformed agents who seek to prevent unlawful entry along the southern and northern border. The new Bureau of Immigration and Customs Enforcement (BICE) employs investigators, who attempt to find undocumented immigrants inside the United States, and Detention and Removal officers, who detain and seek to deport such individuals. The new Bureau of Citizenship and Immigration Services (BCIS) is where people go, or correspond with, to become U.S. citizens or obtain permission to work or extend their stay in the United States.

Following the terrorist attacks of September 11, 2001, the Department of Justice adopted several measures that did not require new legislation to be passed by Congress. Some of these measures created controversy and raised concerns about civil liberties. For example, FBI and INS agents detained for months more than 1,000 foreign nationals of Middle Eastern descent and refused to release the names of the individuals. It is alleged that the Department of Justice adopted tactics that discouraged the detainees from obtaining legal assistance. The Department of Justice also began requiring foreign nationals from primarily Muslim nations to be fingerprinted and questioned by immigration officers upon entry or if they have been living in the United States.

A protester declares her opposition to new rules requiring that men living in the United States who entered on temporary visas and were born in predominantly Muslim nations register with U.S. immigration authorities. Critics charged that the rules unfairly discriminated against residents of Middle Eastern origin.

The Current State of U.S. Immigration

Today, the annual rate of legal immigration is lower than that at earlier periods in U.S. history. For example, from 1901 to 1910 approximately 10.4 immigrants per 1,000 U.S. residents came to the United States. Today, the annual rate is about 3.5 immigrants per 1,000 U.S. residents. While the percentage of foreign-born people in the U.S. population has risen above 11 percent, it remains lower than the 13 percent or higher that prevailed in the country from 1860 to 1930. Still, as has been the case previously in U.S. history, some people argue that even legal immigration should be lowered. These people maintain that immigrants take jobs native-born Americans could fill and that U.S. population growth, to which immigration contributes, harms the environment. In 1996 Congress voted against efforts to reduce legal immigration.

Most immigrants (800,000 to one million annually) enter the United States legally. But over the years the undocumented (illegal) portion of the population has increased to about 2.8 percent of the U.S. population—approximately 8 million people in all.

Today, the legal immigration system in the United States contains many rules, permitting only individuals who fit into certain categories to immigrate—and in many cases only after waiting anywhere from 1 to 10 years or more, depending on the demand in that category. The system, representing a compromise among family, employment, and human rights concerns, has the following elements:

> A U.S. citizen may sponsor for immigration a spouse, parent, sibling, or minor or adult child.
>
> A lawful permanent resident (green card holder) may sponsor only a spouse or child.
>
> A foreign national may immigrate if he or she gains an employer sponsor.
>
> An individual who can show that he or she has a "well-founded fear of persecution" may come to the country as a refugee—or be allowed to stay as an asylee (someone who receives asylum).

Beyond these categories, essentially the only other way to immigrate is to apply for and receive one of the "diversity" visas, 50,000 of which are granted annually by lottery to people from "underrepresented" countries.

In 1996 changes to the law prohibited nearly all incoming immigrants from being eligible for federal public benefits, such as welfare, during their first five years in the country. Refugees were mostly excluded from these changes. In addition, families who sponsor relatives must sign an affidavit of support showing they can financially take care of an immigrant who falls on hard times.

A Short History of Canadian Immigration

In the 1800s, immigration into Canada was largely unrestrict-ed. Farmers and artisans from England and Ireland made up a significant portion of 19th-century immigrants. England's Parliament passed laws that facilitated and encouraged the voyage to North America, particularly for the poor.

After the United States barred Chinese railroad workers from settling in the country, Canada encouraged the immigration of Chinese laborers to assist in the building of Canadian railways. Responding to the racial views of the time, however, the Canadian Parliament began charging a "head tax" for Chinese and South Asian (Indian) immigrants in 1885. The fee of $50—later raised to $500—was well beyond the means of laborers making one or two dollars a day. Later, the government sought additional ways to prohibit Asians from entering the country. For example, it decided to require a "continuous journey," meaning that immigrants to Canada had to travel from their country on a boat that made an uninterrupted passage. For

The government of Prime Minister Lester Pearson, in a policy statement issued in 1966, stressed the importance of immigrants to Canada's economic prospects.

Refuge for a Refugee

Mamoon Jarrah's name aptly sums up his life story: In Arabic, Mamoon means "take refuge"; Jarrah translates to "the surgeon."

Jarrah was only two years old when he and his family were forced to leave Akkar, Palestine (now Akko, Israel), as a result of the 1948 Israeli-Arab war. They lived in Lebanon for two years before moving to Syria. "His father was an educated man, a mechanical engineer, but as refugees, the family lost everything," says Samar Jarrah, his wife. "As a child, Mamoon realized he was different from his wealthy Syrian class-mates because they did not go to the relief agency for rations." He was intelligent, athletic, and popular, but Jarrah's refugee status held him back; because he did not have a passport, for instance, he could not travel to other countries for sports competitions.

Jarrah went to college and then to medical school in Syria, earning his M.D. and completing a residency in anesthesiology. When a medical school professor expressed his belief that the American medical system was superior to the European system, Jarrah and several classmates decided they wanted to study in the United States. They hired a tutor to teach them English, learning enough of the language to take the medical school entrance exams. Jarrah passed the exams and came to the United States on a student visa in 1973. At first, the young doctor strug-gled a bit: his English was limited, he had a new culture to get used to, and, as a student, he found that money was often tight. But he complet-ed an internship, a surgical residency, and a fellowship program in peripheral vascular surgery in New Jersey. Jarrah then received fellow-ship training in cardiovascular surgery in South Carolina and completed a residency in cardiovascular and thoracic surgery in Mississippi.

Jarrah originally intended to return to Syria. His father had passed away soon after he came to the United States, and as the eldest son, he felt responsible for his family. (Eventually, his mother and two of his brothers also came to the United States.) However, as a Palestinian refugee with-out a passport, he would have had difficulty making a living as a physi-cian in Syria. "He thought, 'Why say no to all the rights of being an American citizen?'" says his wife.

Jarrah, once a refugee with no rights, did become an American citizen. Since 1985 he has had a practice in vascular and thoracic surgery in Port Charlotte, Florida. "His journey to America has been emotionally draining, and there were times when he wondered if he would make it," says Samar Jarrah. "But now he has absolute freedom."

immigrants or asylum seekers from Asia, this was nearly impossible.

As the 20th century progressed, concerns about race led to further restrictions on immigration to Canada. These restrictions particularly hurt Jewish and other refugees seeking to flee persecution in Europe. Government statistics indicate that Canada accepted no more than 5,000 Jewish refugees before and during the Holocaust.

After World War II, Canada, like the United States, began accepting thousands of Europeans displaced by the war. Canada's laws were modified to accept these war refugees, as well as Hungarians fleeing Communist authorities after the crushing of the 1956 Hungarian Revolution.

The Immigration Act of 1952 in Canada allowed for a "tap on, tap off" approach to immigration, granting administrative authorities the power to allow more immigrants into the country in good economic times, and fewer in times of recession. The shortcoming of such an approach is that there is little evidence immigrants harm a national economy and much evidence they contribute to economic growth, particularly in the growth of the labor force.

In 1966 the government of Prime Minister Lester Pearson introduced a policy statement stressing how immigrants were key to Canada's economic growth. With Canada's relatively small population base, it became clear that in the absence of newcomers, the country would not be able to grow. The policy was introduced four years after Parliament enacted important legislation that eliminated Canada's own version of racially based national-origin quotas.

In 1967 a new law established a points system that awarded entry to potential immigrants using criteria based primarily on an individual's age, language ability, skills, education, family relationships, and job prospects. The total points needed for entry of an immigrant is set by the Minister of Citizenship and Immigration Canada. The new law also established a category for humanitarian (refugee) entry.

The 1976 Immigration Act refined and expanded the possibility for entry under the points system, particularly for those seeking to sponsor family members. The act also expanded refugee and asylum law to comport with Canada's international obligations. The law established five basic categories for immigration into Canada: 1) family; 2) humanitarian; 3) independents (including skilled workers), who immigrate to Canada on their own; 4) assisted relatives; and 5) business immigrants (including investors, entrepreneurs, and the self-employed).

The new Immigration and Refugee Protection Act, which took effect June 28, 2002, made a series of modifications to existing Canadian immigration law. The act, and the regulations that followed, toughened rules on those seeking asylum and the process for removing people unlawfully in Canada.

The law modified the points system, adding greater flexibility for skilled immigrants and temporary workers to become permanent residents, and evaluating skilled workers on the weight of their transferable skills as well as those of their specific occupation. The legislation also made it easier for employers to have a labor shortage declared in an industry or sector, which would facilitate the entry of foreign workers in that industry or sector.

On family immigration, the act permitted parents to sponsor dependent children up to the age of 22 (previously 19 was the maximum age at which a child could be sponsored for immigration). The act also allowed partners in common-law arrangements, including same-sex partners, to be considered as family members for the purpose of immigration sponsorship. Along with these liberalizing measures, the act also included provisions to address perceived gaps in immigration-law enforcement.

Push and Pull Factors for Middle Eastern Immigrants

Middle Easterners have been coming to the United States since the late 1800s. Over time, particularly since the second half of the 20th century, economics has been less of a motivating factor for emigration, as education, politics, and the desire for certain freedoms (especially religious freedoms) have taken greater precedence. And while many of the early immigrants were Christians, the number of Muslims coming to North America from the Middle East has increased significantly in the past few decades.

The first wave of Middle Eastern immigrants came from modern-day Lebanon, Syria, Jordan, and Israel (including Palestinians). They emigrated primarily for economic opportunities and to escape religious persecution. In sociological terms, they were motivated to come to North America because of both "push" and "pull" factors. Push factors are problems within the homeland, such as civil war, religious or political persecution, poverty, and famine. Pull factors attract people to

Arab demonstrators in Amman, Jordan, call for a jihad, or holy war, against Israel, August 1969. Conflict in the region has been a major "push" factor, spurring many people to emigrate.

a country: civil liberties, employment and educational opportunities, the desire to be with family, and so on. When the push-pull factors are weak, there's little incentive for migration. For example, relatively few people immigrate to North America from wealthy Middle Eastern countries such as Bahrain, Oman, and Qatar.

What were some of the push and pull factors for early Middle Eastern immigrants? According to Michael W. Suleiman, editor of *Arabs in America: Building a New Future*, the Greater Syrian economy was hit hard in the mid-1800s with the emergence of Japan as competition in the silk industry, and again at the end of the century, when a blight took its toll on vineyards. During the late 1800s, Christians faced oppression from the Ottoman regime, which pitted them against Muslims. While not well off, Arab Muslims had a higher social status than Christians. "The threat of losing that 'high' status made many Muslims susceptible to suggestions from local Ottoman rulers that their Christian neighbors were the cause of rather than companions in their troubles," notes Suleiman. "The worsened social and economic conditions in Syria in the mid-1800s and the beginning of the disintegration of feudalism, especially among the Druze, produced social turmoil that erupted in sectarian riots in which thousands of Christians perished." Many Maronite Christians, in particular, chose to flee to the United States for what they thought would be a temporary stay.

For the most part, these early immigrants didn't want to establish deep roots in America; they earned money by peddling, working in restaurants, and doing crochet and lace work. But after World War I, Suleiman explains, that attitude changed. "It became clear to large numbers of Arabs in North America that it was not possible to go 'home' again and that the United States and Canada were their homes."

In *The History of Arab Immigration to the U.S.*, sociologist Louise Cainker explains some of the recent motivations for Arab immigration. Two pull factors, education and reuniting with family members, are common to many of the countries. For other immigrants, however, jobs are the primary motivator to come to North America. "Some 90 percent of Yemeni immigrants," Cainker notes, "are unaccompanied men who came to the U.S. to work, save money, and support their families in Yemen."

A spike in Middle Eastern immigration to the United States followed the 1991 Gulf War. In the 1980s, according to U.S. immigration data, 19,533 Iraqis had immigrated to the United States; during the 1990s, that number more than doubled, to 40,749. In the wake of the Gulf War, Kurds in northern Iraq and Shia Muslims in the southern part of the country rose up in an attempt to overthrow the regime of Saddam Hussein. The uprisings were brutally suppressed, and hundreds of thousands of Iraqis the regime suspected of disloyalty were arrested, tortured, and, in many cases, murdered. Even those whose safety was not immediately threatened had reason to want to leave Iraq. Because of the regime's failure to comply with disarmament provisions contained in the Gulf War cease-fire agreement, the international community imposed economic sanctions on

Allied troops examine the remains of an Iraqi Scud missile during the 1991 Persian Gulf War. The war, plus subsequent Kurdish and Shiite uprisings and years of crippling economic sanctions, combined to produce a spike in Iraqi immigration to North America in the 1990s.

This angry exchange—between an Israeli policeman and a Palestinian blocked from worshiping at the Al-Aqsa Mosque in Jerusalem—took place in 2000, during an extended period of deadly violence in the West Bank and Gaza Strip. The turmoil led to a large exodus of Palestinian Christians from the occupied territories.

Iraq. Those sanctions further devastated the country's economy and impoverished millions of Iraqis during the 1990s.

But the effects of the war and the international economic sanctions imposed on Iraq in its aftermath were not confined to Iraqi citizens. For example, many Yemeni and Palestinian workers who had been employed in Iraq lost their jobs. Some turned to North America for work opportunities, a trend reflected in immigration statistics: during the 1980s, 5,474 Yemenis had come to the United States; in the 1990s, 16,319 arrived.

Palestinians had to contend not only with the loss of employment opportunities in Iraq, but also with dim prospects in the West Bank and Gaza Strip. Although the Oslo Accords, signed in 1993, had established a framework by which Israel might permit the creation of an independent Palestinian state, mistrust and violence soon derailed the agreement. By 1996 a bombing campaign by Palestinian extremists had prompted the Israeli government to impose periodic border restrictions and curfews, which crippled the Palestinian economy. Many Palestinians who had come to the United States to study for careers in industry and technology were forced to reevaluate their plans to return to the Middle East. "It was for these jobs that Palestinians sought an education in the U.S.," says Cainker. "When they became unavailable, they had no option but to stay and work in the U.S. Returning home was impossible due to Israeli restrictions on Palestinian residency and work." Still, Cainker believes, "one might expect Palestinian immigration to be even higher than it is . . . But counterbalancing this push factor has been a Palestinian determination to stay on their land so it would not be confiscated by the Israeli government."

Emigration from Israel

In the 18 centuries between Rome's suppression of the Bar Kochba Rebellion in 135 and the establishment of the State of Israel in 1948, Jews settled all over the world. The Diaspora—as the totality of Jews living outside Palestine is called—included significant communities in the United States and Canada. Even today, more Jews live in the United States than in Israel.

Today migration between Israel and North America is a complex, two-way process, as Gallya Lahav and Asher Arian note in their article "Israelis in a Jewish Diaspora: The Multiple Dilemmas of a Globalized Group." Using Israeli emigration data as their source, Lahav and Arian detected several trends: "a continuing stream of Israeli immigrants to the U.S., a rise in the number of Israelis returning to Israel to live, and the emergence of a new category of 'transnationals'—individuals with footholds in both the United States and Israel."

In her book *Kibbutzniks in the Diaspora*, Naama Sabar describes some of the "push-pull factors" that contribute to Israeli emigration. "The main pull factors cited are financial prospects, better job opportunities, first-order family ties in the

United States . . . and more rapid upward mobility (mainly achieved through higher education). For some, push factors include the economic and political situation in Israel, though not the security situation per se; wars which result in greater solidarity (e.g., the Six-Day War) tend to lower the tendency to emigrate."

The Jewish Israelis who come to the United States might stay temporarily or seek citizenship, but many are from the wealthier sector. "The majority of Israeli emigrants can no longer be described as marginal members of society, or 'weaklings,'" write Lahav and Arian.

Meanwhile, an escalation of violence in the West Bank and the Gaza Strip beginning in 2000 sparked the emigration of a large number of Christians from those areas. Many headed to the United States or Canada. One Palestinian Authority adviser on Christians and church affairs estimated that the number of Christians in the West Bank declined from 35,000 in 1997 to 25,000 in 2002, noted Dr. Daphne Tsimhoni in her article "Christians Fleeing Palestinian Controlled Areas."

Immigrants from Sudan

There's a new type of migration occurring among Sudanese, believes Rogaia Mustafa Abusharaf, author of *Wanderings: Sudanese Migrants and Exiles in North America*. "For unlike border crossings to Kenya, Uganda, or Zaire, which is dominated by war-ravaged southern Sudanese, or to the Persian Gulf states, which are dominated by Arabic-speaking Muslim northerners, North American migration represents a cross-section of Sudanese from almost every ethnicity, region, and religion. . . . For the first time in the history of Sudanese population mobility, we witness a movement that is diverse as the country itself," Abusharaf writes.

During the 1990s, Abusharaf conducted a survey of 300 Sudanese immigrants to North America. About half of those surveyed came after 1980. Among the reasons for migration, education or social mobility was the most common, cited by

39 percent of the survey respondents; 21 percent said they were motivated by political reasons, and 20 percent cited economic factors.

Of the Sudanese who immigrated for political reasons, the overwhelming majority—82 percent—came from the southern region, which suffered greatly under the efforts of Sudan's Arab- and Muslim-dominated government to stamp out a rebellion and impose Islamic rule on the entire country. The residents of southern Sudan are primarily black Africans and practice indigenous religions or Christianity, but Islamic studies are part of the school curriculum, and all citizens must follow the Islamic dress code. In the face of the harassment, discrimination, and even violent acts committed against them because of their religious beliefs—not to mention their country's long-running civil war and chronic famine—many Coptic Christians from the south

By 2002 Sudan's civil war, which broke out in 1983, had displaced as many as 4.4 million people. About 400,000, including this Sudanese family, had left their homeland to live abroad.

decided to pursue a new life in North America. As one Sudanese Copt explains, "hundreds of Coptic families . . . came to the United States and Canada to escape extremism."

Changing Demographics

For many years Middle Eastern immigrants were overwhelmingly Christian. With the most recent arrivals, however, a larger percentage are adherents of Islam.

Writing in the summer 2001 issue of the *Middle East Quarterly*, journalist Alexander Rose states, "Prior to 1965 . . . only small numbers of Muslims lived in the United States; and there was little communal activity, owing mostly to their own lack of education and a worry about provoking prejudice. After 1965, however, because the immigration act of that year laid down a preference for professionals, scientists, and artists of 'exceptional ability,' the Muslim community benefited from an influx of educated, talented individuals who quickly developed financial muscle."

While the number of Middle Eastern Muslim immigrants has increased, Christians still constitute the vast majority of Arab Americans, according to a 2000 Zogby International poll. Specifically, the poll found that 42 percent of Arab Americans are Catholic, 23 percent are Orthodox Christian, and 12 percent are Protestant; by comparison, just 23 percent are Muslim.

Regarding ancestry, nearly half (47 percent) of Arab Americans are of Lebanese descent, according to the Arab American Institute. An additional 15 percent are Syrian, 9 percent are Egyptian, 6 percent are Palestinian, 3 percent are Iraqi, and 2 percent are Jordanian; the remaining 18 percent fall into the "other" category.

The Diversity Lottery

Foreigners wishing to enter the United States need to obtain a visa. There are many types of visas, but they fall into two broad categories: immigrant (for permanent residence) and non-immigrant (for work, travel, or study on a temporary basis). For countries with low immigration rates to the United States, Section 203 (c) of the Immigration and Nationality Act established the Diversity Immigrant Visa Lottery. Each year, the government makes available 55,000 permanent resident visas—5,000 of which are reserved for the Nicaraguan and Central American Relief Act—through a lottery drawing.

As with any lottery, there are many players but relatively few winners. According to the U.S. Department of State, of the 6.2 million qualified applicants for the 2003 lottery, 87,000 were selected randomly to be in the lottery pool. Still, the "payoff" is worth the long odds: permanent resident status and the ability to bring a husband or wife and any unmarried children under the age of 21 to the United States. The 2003 lottery pool included many people from the Middle East, among them 768 Iranians, 1,629 Turks, 75 Jordanians, and 145 Israelis.

Middle Eastern Immigration to Canada

As was the case with the United States, Canada began receiving Middle Eastern immigrants in the late 1800s. At times in those early years, however, the response to some Middle Easterners, like Canadian winters, was somewhat chilly. "Around the turn of the century, there were fears that these Arab-origin immigrants, along with immigrants from Asia and Eastern and Southern Europe, would negatively affect Canada's Anglo-Saxon heritage and white European master project," write Sharon McIrvin Abu-Laban and Baha Abu-Laban in *Arabs in America: Building a New Future*. "Consequently, Arab immigrants faced serious barriers in their admission, were characterized harshly by ranking officials of the time, and were viewed as difficult to assimilate into the Canadian ideal."

Today, immigrants are recognized as being essential to Canada's future, and because of that, Canada has put out the welcome mat. In 2002 the Honorable Denis Coderre, Minister of Citizenship and Immigration, predicted that immigrants would be the sole source of Canada's population growth by the year 2026. Fifteen years sooner, by 2011, newcomers to

Denis Coderre, Canada's Minister of Citizenship and Immigration, predicted in 2002 that immigrants would account for all of his country's population growth within a quarter century.

Canada are expected to account for all of the growth in the country's labor force. With its future tied so closely to immigrants, Canada extends a hand of friendship to all newcomers. The government encourages its citizens to volunteer in a Host Program, in which they show new immigrants around their community, help them become familiar with local businesses and schools, and introduce them to Canadian culture.

More than 300,000 Canadians are of Arab descent. Most of them live in the provinces of Ontario and Quebec. Nearly half of the Arab Canadians are of Lebanese descent, and 6 out of 10 are Christian.

In her book *Saffron Sky: A Life Between Iran and America*, Iranian American journalist Gelareh Asayesh explained why her parents, who immigrated to the United States from Iran in 1977, eventually settled in Canada. "In Canada, where immigrants were not the problem they had become in the United States, and where the Iranian hostage crisis was not a personal affront, my parents felt welcome in a way they had not in America," Asayesh said. "Winnipeg offered a warm and friendly Iranian community. . . . Canada offered my parents what the United States never had: the promise of permanence."

4 Making a New Life

Middle Eastern immigrants often live in the traditional havens for newcomers—large cities such as New York, Los Angeles, and Toronto. On the other hand, because education is a common pull factor, it's not unusual to find small Middle Eastern enclaves near college towns. According to the Arab American Institute, one-third of Arab Americans live in New York, California, or Michigan. New Jersey and Virginia are two other states with sizable Middle Eastern communities.

Notable Middle Eastern Communities in the United States

Perhaps the most well known hub for Middle Eastern Americans is metropolitan Detroit, especially Dearborn, Michigan, which is located southwest of the Motor City. Today, an estimated 250,000 Arab Americans live in the Detroit-Dearborn area. About 20 percent of Dearborn's 97,000 residents are Arab Americans.

Detroit's Arab American community dates back to the late 1800s, when some of the first Middle Eastern immigrants to the United States, primarily Lebanese men, worked as peddlers. As the automobile industry developed and grew in the early 20th century, however, many Arab immigrants found work in the factories. (These jobs were more plentiful for immigrants because of the Ford Motor Company's policy against hiring

◄ Students of the American Islamic Academy in Dearborn, Michigan, attend a banquet. During the early part of the 20th century, Arab immigrants were attracted to Dearborn (headquarters of the Ford Motor Company) by well-paying jobs in the automobile industry. Today the Detroit-Dearborn area is home to one of the nation's largest and most important Arab American communities.

blacks to work in its auto plants.) "The Arab American community gradually concentrated in the Dearborn row houses constructed by Henry Ford, literally in the shadows of the Rouge plant," writes Karen Rignall in "Building an Arab-American Community in Dearborn," an article published in the *Journal of the International Institute*.

Over the years, people from other Middle Eastern countries have come to southeast Michigan: Yemenis, Syrians, Palestinians, and many more. "Each wave of arrivals adds another layer to the rich history of this heterogeneous community," says Rignall. "Arab immigrants hope Dearborn will offer chances of finding work. They also look to Dearborn for social networks, mosques and churches where they may pray in a familiar manner, stores where they may buy the clothes they prefer and the foods they grew up with: in sum, a cultural milieu that dulls the edges of the experience of dislocation and adjustment."

New York City, a magnet for immigrants from all over the world, is home to a sizable community of Syrian Jews. Estimates of the number of New York residents in this somewhat unusual Arab-Jewish group range from 20,000 to 70,000; it's difficult to pinpoint a precise figure because Syrian Jews don't usually identify themselves as Arabs or Jewish Arabs. While many Syrian Jews live in Brooklyn's Flatbush and Bensonhurst neighborhoods, some have migrated to New Jersey.

The casual observer wouldn't notice much, if any, difference between the Syrian Jews and other Jewish groups in Brooklyn, according to Walter P. Zenner, who has studied this community since the late 1950s. "But there are ways in which they have in the past and continue today to maintain aspects of their Middle Eastern heritage," writes Zenner in *A Community of Many Worlds: Arab Americans in New York City*.

Of particular note is the music in their services. "The most Arab of cultural forms for Syrian Jews in Brooklyn is paradoxically one of the most Jewish," says Zenner. "The Syrian Jewish community has preserved Arab music for use with Hebrew

More Iranians live in the Los Angeles area than anywhere else in the world outside of Iran—leading some expatriates to dub their adopted hometown "Tehrangeles."

songs and prayers. . . . The liturgical music of the Aleepan synagogue follows Arab musical modes called *maqamaat*. One particular mode, *sikah*, is used for most Sabbath services and for the Torah reading." As Zenner concludes, "The Arabic musical tradition is preserved and taught to new generations through the synagogue service."

Another important Middle Eastern enclave is in Los Angeles. In fact, L.A. contains the largest concentration of Iranians in the world outside of Iran itself. An estimated 600,000 Iranians live in southern California; many of them immigrated around the time of Iran's Islamic Revolution in 1979. According to an Associated Press article, "Iranians Make Home in L.A.," the tastes and sounds of Iran are found easily in the city some

Iranian Americans refer to as "Tehrangeles." "Along Westwood Boulevard and in the San Fernando Valley, signs in Farsi's delicate, cursive script advertise Persian market rug merchants, restaurants serving a staple rice-and-meat dish called chello kebab and grocery stores stocking biranyi paste, lavash bread and halva, a nougat made with sesame seeds," the article reports. Although immigrants might find these familiar things comforting, one young Iranian American notes that the youth "love anything that's American."

Working in America

Middle Eastern immigrants tend to be well educated—nearly 50 percent have a bachelor's degree—and they are represented in virtually every field, including medicine, education, finance, the arts, and the automobile industry. It was the auto industry that drew many of the first wave of Arab immigrants to the greater Detroit area. Some have made the transition from line workers to labor officials. The late Stephen Yokich, who served two terms as president of the United Auto Workers, was of Arab descent.

Like other immigrants, many Middle Eastern newcomers are self-employed. Some Middle Eastern businesses have grown into large, well-known enterprises, such as the Haggar Clothing Company or the Maloof Companies, which, among other ventures, owns the NBA Sacramento Kings and the WNBA Sacramento Monarchs. But other Middle Eastern businesses are small: mom-and-pop stores, gas stations, restaurants.

Home Away from Home

Being a recently arrived immigrant and being the new kid in school have something in common: It helps to have someone show the way around. For some Middle Eastern immigrants, that someone will be a family member.

Community organizations also can play an important role. In Dearborn, the Arab Community Center for Economic and Social Services (ACCESS) serves about 45,000 people each year.

From Her Kitchen to Yours

As a girl growing up in Baghdad, Iraq, Nawal Nasrallah loved the smells wafting from her family's and her neighbors' kitchens. Today, she helps bring those aromas into American kitchens. She is the author of *Delights from the Garden of Eden: A Cookbook and a History of the Iraqi Cuisine*, a compilation of recipes and food-related stories from Mesopotamia, an area that gave rise to some of the world's oldest civilizations.

An accomplished cook and a thorough researcher, Nasrallah shares traditional recipes such as appetizers, vegetarian dishes, and desserts. The book also has an ample dash of Iraqi history and culture. For example, it explains that Italian cannoli, a tubular pastry shell filled with sweetened ricotta cheese, has culinary ancestors: a 10th-century Iraqi sweet called *halaqeem* and a 13th-century treat known as *qanawat*—literally, "a tube."

Nasrallah presents a culinary journey in her cookbook, but her personal journey to the United States is even more compelling. Her husband, Shakir Mustafa, came to North America in 1990 to earn his doctorate; the family, Nasrallah and three children—Shamam, Iba, and Bilal—planned to join him soon afterward. The day they were to leave, however, Iraqi soldiers invaded Kuwait. Shamam, as an 18-year-old male, was forced to stay behind, but the others managed to get a ride with a truck driver to Amman, Jordan. From there they flew to New York and, ultimately, to Indiana, where Mustafa was studying. After about a year, Shamam was able to rejoin the family.

Nasrallah, who was a professor of English literature before coming to the United States, worked as a seamstress to support the family, but she never lost her interest in research and food.

In 1996 tragedy struck the family. Bilal, the youngest child, suffered a fatal brain hemorrhage. The cookbook was a way for Nasrallah to work through the loss of her 13-year-old son.

On a broader level, notes Nasrallah, the book introduces Iraq's cuisine and its rich cultural traditions to Westerners, including second- and third-generation Iraqi Americans. After the 1991 Gulf War, many families left Iraq, she says, which gave rise to a whole generation growing up away from their home country. Many of them are not able to read Arabic, and yet they need to know something about their heritage. "This is where my cookbook comes in," she says, adding that her daughter, Iba, a lawyer, used to call her and ask how to prepare her favorite traditional dishes. That was not easy, given the lengthy explanations required. "Now, I tell her what page to turn to in my book, and spend the rest of the call chatting."

ACCESS "started off helping men find industrial jobs by teaching them the English words for wrench, hammer, nail, saw, and other tools," according to an article in the April 2003 issue of the magazine *Washington Report on Middle East Affairs.* "Next it gave Arab women English lessons. Before long ACCESS was providing all kinds of human services, including helping immigrants start small businesses and navigate the school, banking, health care and social and civil systems most Americans take for granted." ACCESS, which won a Points of Light Award in 1992, has an extensive cultural arts program as well. One of its largest endeavors, the Arab American National Museum, was scheduled to open in 2004.

Iranian immigration to the United States skyrocketed in the aftermath of the 1979 Islamic Revolution.

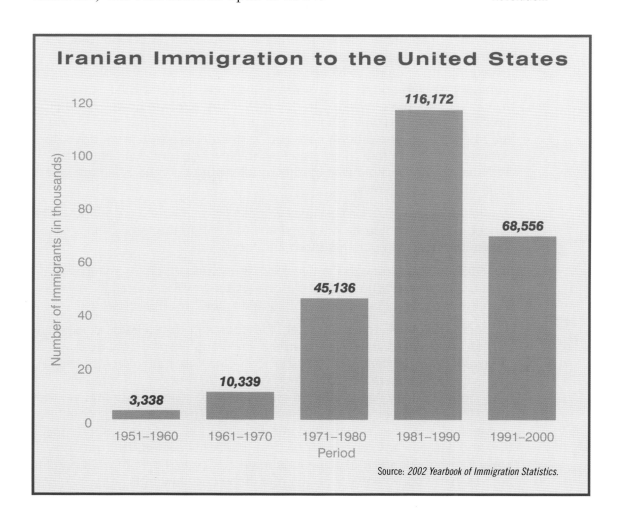

Iranian Immigration to the United States

Number of Immigrants (in thousands)

- 1951–1960: 3,338
- 1961–1970: 10,339
- 1971–1980: 45,136
- 1981–1990: 116,172
- 1991–2000: 68,556

Period

Source: *2002 Yearbook of Immigration Statistics.*

In addition to family and community centers, the synagogues, churches, and mosques that serve communities with large Middle Eastern immigrant populations often take on a dual role: religious center and socialization outlet. In "Expressions of Islam in America," Gisela Webb, a professor of religious studies, notes that some mosques, much like some urban ethnic churches, "function as centers for learning and sharing information about surviving in America as much as they are centers for prayer."

5 Fitting In

Assimilation, in simple terms, is the process by which a person from one culture takes on the mind-set, habits, and customs of another culture. While Arab Americans have generally done very well for themselves, noted scholar Michael Suleiman believes that they still haven't been fully accepted in the United States. "True integration and full assimilation have eluded them," Suleiman asserts in *Arabs in America: Building a New Future*.

Like some Arabs in North America, some Israelis have not assimilated into the larger society—and don't want to. In her article "The New Immigrants: A Contemporary Profile," Rina Cohen examines Israelis living in Canada. Cohen suggests that Israeli Canadians "feel guilty for leaving their homeland and express significant ambivalence about their presence in Canada. Most of them foster a dream to return to Israel one day. Thus, they make no visible efforts to assimilate into the culture of the country in which they live, or even into that of the native Jewish community."

In fact, Cohen notes, Israeli Jews in Toronto "have deliberately distanced themselves from the highly organized Jewish community, constituting an Israeli ethnic group in the city." Perhaps some of this desire to remain separate from the larger Jewish community reflects the differing attitudes toward religion held by Israeli immigrants: whereas Canadian Jews,

◀ An Arab American family at the dinner table. The experiences and attitudes of Middle Eastern immigrants are likely to differ markedly from those of their North American–born children—and typically the grandchildren of immigrants are fully assimilated into Canadian or American culture.

Cohen observes, tend to emphasize the religious significance of Judaism, Israeli immigrants tend to have a more nationalistic view of what it means to be Jewish. "In order to escape both assimilation and religiosity, Israelis take action to maintain cultural connections with Israel and other Israelis," notes Cohen.

Naama Sabar studied an interesting subset of Israeli immigrants: kibbutzniks living in Los Angeles. (A kibbutz is a communal settlement in Israel; the people who live in a kibbutz are called kibbutzniks.) The kibbutzniks don't fit the typical profile of Israeli American immigrants: they're not as well-off or as educated, they tend to be self-employed, and the women work outside the home.

Kibbutzniks are not exempt from problems such as culture shock or language difficulties, Sabar notes; they just handle these challenges differently from other immigrants. "What helps them cope with the changes in their lives is the highly developed social network which serves as a security net, a mechanism of survival. This social network is characterized by multiple, intense, substantial personal links based on friendship, interdependence, and mutual background, rather than the official organizations which characterize other immigrant groups in the United States," observes Sabar in her book *Kibbutzniks in the Diaspora*. "The kibbutzniks cope with their foreignness by creating an 'island of estrangement.'"

Arguably, assimilation can be somewhat easier for immigrants who came to North America because they wanted to than for those who felt they had no choice but to immigrate. Many Palestinians fall into the latter group. "Palestine, the homeland and the nostalgic village, is alive in Palestinian memories and viewed as the utopian solution," writes May Seikaly in *Arabs in America: Building a New Future*. "On the whole, this community sees itself as transplanted, forced into exile by conditions beyond its control. To mitigate the effect of this alienation, Palestinians in America transplant the lifestyle of the old country. . . . They surround themselves with the artifacts of the culture: embroideries, the mounted religious drawings and

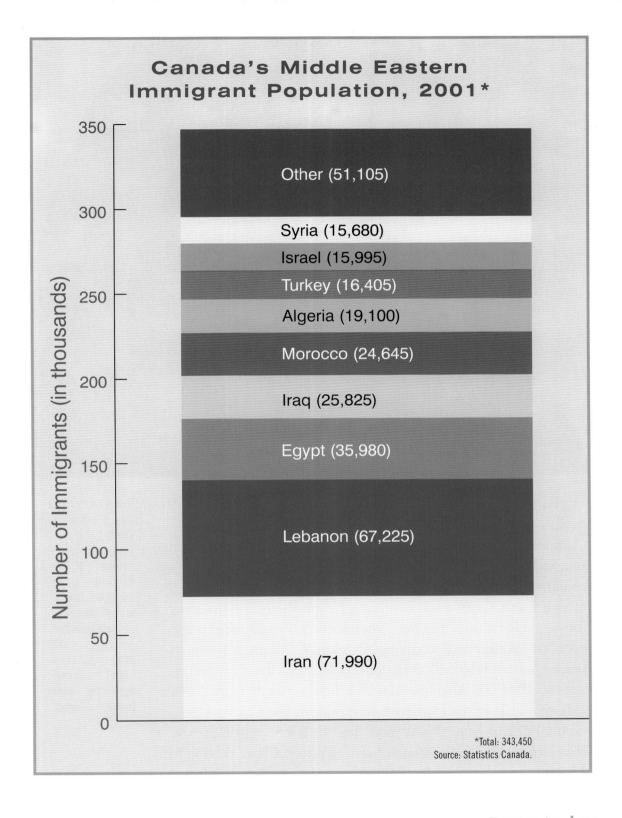

Canada's Middle Eastern Immigrant Population, 2001*

Number of Immigrants (in thousands)

Other (51,105)

Syria (15,680)

Israel (15,995)

Turkey (16,405)

Algeria (19,100)

Morocco (24,645)

Iraq (25,825)

Egypt (35,980)

Lebanon (67,225)

Iran (71,990)

*Total: 343,450
Source: Statistics Canada.

scripts, the sounds of Arabic music and language, and the smells of Arab food."

Similarly, Iranian culture is emotionally binding and nationalistic, says Ali Akbar Mahdi in "The Second Generation Iranians: Questions and Concerns." However, "while the Iranian immigrants often express a strong desire for preservation of their cultural heritage, they show no resistance to the forces of assimilation to the host society." Although Iranian Americans are relatively large in number and live in major cities such as Los Angeles, Mahdi believes that "it is still too early to speak of the Iranian community in the U.S. as a national phenomenon" and says that "it is not very clear to what extent the Iranians have been able to transfer their cultural heritage to their children."

Some Westerners view the *hijab* as a symbol of the repression women endure in Middle Eastern Islamic societies. But many Muslim women disagree, and they continue to wear the traditional headscarf even after moving to North America.

Age to Age

Mahdi raises an important point: the experiences of immigrants and their children (and grandchildren and great-grandchildren) vary significantly. People who emigrated from their country of birth as adults—referred to as first-generation immigrants—typically have a more difficult time adapting to life in their new country than do children born in the new country (referred to as the second generation). For example, a Sudanese couple who immigrate to the United States in their twenties may have difficulty mastering the English language or learning the nuances of Western culture. But their American-born children will almost inevitably learn English in school and absorb American attitudes and customs from their peers—even if their parents continue to speak Nubian and observe other Sudanese customs at home. In turn, the third generation (the grandchildren of the original immigrants) will probably be even more "Americanized"; indeed, they may have little if any knowledge of, or interest in, the "old country." As Mahdi notes, "While the first generation immigrants make every effort to maintain the native language and culture, the second generation's efforts in learning parental language and culture are very limited and half-hearted. The third generation's efforts in this regard are very minimal and symbolic. By fourth generation, little of a grandparent's cultural heritage can be found."

In many ways, members of the "1.5 generation"—as those who immigrate (usually with their parents) during childhood or the early teen years are sometimes called—encounter the most vexing situations from a cultural standpoint. They are, in a sense, between two cultures. One young Iranian American describes it this way: "They have a word in Persian, 'do-hava.' It means 'two-weathered.' You're not completely American and not completely Iranian."

East vs. West

The Arab Americans who have recently immigrated to the United States are quite different from those who came 100 years ago. The first arrivals typically desired to fit in with the American way of life; that's not necessarily so with today's newcomers. Yvonne Yazbeck Haddad, in *A Community of Many Worlds: Arab Americans in New York City*, notes, "The new immigrants tend to be more ethnically conscious, have

Fascinating Rhythms

When Scott Marcus's orchestra members begin to play, the distinctive sounds of the *ud* and *saz*; *nay*; and *qanun* and *santur* fill the air, with the *dumbek*, *darabukkah*, and *zarb* keeping the beat. These Arab and Turkish lutes, reed flutes, plucked and hammered zithers, and percussion instruments, respectively, do more than play Middle Eastern music; in the hands of Marcus's Middle East Ensemble, they promote cultural harmony.

The Middle East Ensemble at the University of California–Santa Barbara—America's largest Middle Eastern orchestra—includes a chorus and a dance troupe. A few of the Ensemble's 60-plus members are from the Middle East, but most are Americans. Their concerts draw from a rich and diverse well of Arab, Armenian, Persian, Turkish, and Greek music and dance, from folk songs to modern tunes to classical music. "And yet classical Middle Eastern music isn't reserved for a few," observes Marcus, an ethnomusicologist who has studied in Egypt and is a professor at UCSB. "It's accessible to everyone and known by people on the street."

Middle Eastern music can't be described in simple terms, says Marcus. For example, there are several types of Egyptian music, and each country's music has its own distinctive rhythm. "The rhythm is part of the cultural identity," he says. While the traditional Western octave has 12 notes, the Middle Eastern octave has 24 notes and includes half flats and half sharps.

The Middle East Ensemble's concerts have reached people as close by as California and as far away as Uzbekistan, where the group performed at the Festival of Eastern Song. Some audiences enjoy the sounds and dances of their homelands; for others, it's a new experience. "The Ensemble's concerts present the diversity and dynamism of Middle Eastern cultures in an entertaining and educational way," says Marcus. "We introduce a dance or a song so that audience members not only listen to or see the performance, but so that they have a better appreciation for the cultural themes. We break down a lot of stereotypes."

more contact with the home country, and in general are more protective of their religious identity."

The clash between Western and Middle Eastern cultures sometimes plays out in the classroom. Paula Hajar, of Columbia University's Teachers College, surveyed Arab American parents and their children's teachers. The teachers expressed concern about gender inequality, corporal punishment, and the Arab mothers' lack of involvement in the schools. From the parents' perspective, teachers were viewed as weak disciplinarians who held low academic expectations for their students. "When a teacher was more concerned with 'being a friend to [the] child' rather than keeping the child in line or making demands on him or her," Hajar notes, "parents were distressed. They did, however, appreciate the American way of teaching to many different abilities and not just attending to the academically gifted, which was often the case in their own countries."

Is Sisterhood Powerful?

Many North Americans believe that in the Islamic societies of the Middle East, women are second-class citizens, oppressed and relegated solely to traditional roles such as wife and mother. Many Middle Eastern women, in turn, believe that this stereotype is inaccurate and unfair. Islam's holy book, the Koran, is fairly straightforward when it comes to the question of women's status in society: woman, it says, "enjoys equal rights to those of man in everything, she stands on an equal footing with men." Yet Arab culture traditionally has accorded men superior status.

Today, the rights and status of Middle Eastern women vary considerably by country. For example, Israel and Turkey, which are not Arab countries, generally guarantee equal rights to women under the law. In Iran, which also is not an Arab country, a woman may not travel abroad or work outside the home without the permission of her husband; when in public Iranian women are required to wear conservative Islamic dress, such as the chador, a dark cloak that covers the entire body except for the face. Women are not permitted to drive a car in Saudi Arabia, vote in Kuwait, or testify in criminal proceedings in Yemen.

One highly visible symbol of the way society's image of women (and women's self-image) differs in Western and Islamic Middle Eastern cultures is the wearing of the traditional head covering, or *hijab*. Muslim women who wear the *hijab* say it's their choice—and a liberating one, at that. "In the Western world, the *hijab* has come to symbolize either forced silence or radical, unconscionable militancy," writes Naheed Mustafa, a Canadian Muslim, in "My Body Is My Own Business." "Actually, it is neither. It is simply a woman's assertion that judgment of her physical person is to play no role whatsoever in social interaction."

Not all Muslim American women share the same feelings about wearing the *hijab*. For his study, Ali Akbar Mahdi surveyed first-generation Iranian American female immigrants: 73 percent said the veil limited movement, and 80 percent strongly disagreed that it was good protection for women. Mahdi's 113-question survey spanned topics from Islamic law to marriage. Overall, concludes Mahdi, while many of these women disagree with the Iranian traditional role of women, few identify themselves as feminists in the Western definition. "Although these women believe in male-female equality and in the opportunities provided to women to enhance their status in society, they are not too enthusiastic about the individualistic demands characterizing Western feminism," Mahdi says.

Ways of the Middle East

Just as Middle Eastern immigrants bring with them long-standing habits, they also preserve the arts and holidays that are important to them. One Middle Eastern art that is treasured and practiced by many immigrants is calligraphy, writing in beautiful, stylized script. There are many forms of Arabic calligraphy, which is written from right to left. Calligraphy has

In Arab cultures calligraphy—ornate, stylized writing—adorns everything from mosques to books.

special significance to Muslims: because of the traditional Islamic prohibition against depicting the human form, calligraphy has been used to adorn everything from books to mosques.

Many Middle Eastern immigrants continue to observe the major holy days of their faith: for Jews, Passover and Yom Kippur; for Muslims, Ramadan, a month of fasting; and for Christians, Christmas and Easter. They may also observe a special new year according to their own calendar, such as Rosh Hashanah for the Jews. Yet, particularly if the immigrants are living apart from others with the same cultural or religious background, a holiday might lose some of its significance.

Iranian American journalist Gelareh Asayesh hadn't observed the Iranian calendar since her teens. But that changed after the birth of her daughter, she writes in *Saffron Sky: A Life Between Iran and America*. Iranian holidays include Charshanbeh-soori, or "festive Wednesday," a farewell to winter; and Sizdah-bedar, observed on the 13th day of the new year, to ward off bad luck. But it's the Iranian New Year, Norooz, that has major significance, complete with presents, parties, and a *haft-sin* (literally, seven objects that begin with the letter *s*). "The *haft-sin*, the functional equivalent of the Christmas tree or the menorah, is a metaphor for life, a collection of symbolic objects laid out for the New Year," Asayesh explains, listing the items and their significance. "Greens and apples and Russian olives for abundance, gold coins for prosperity, hyacinth for beauty, vinegar and garlic for life's bitter moments."

Followers of some Middle Eastern Christian faiths observe St. Barbara's Day in December. As the story is told, Barbara was the daughter of a pagan, Dioscurus, who locked her in a tower and then killed her because of her conversion to Christianity. Upon her death, Dioscurus was stuck by lightning and reduced to a pile of ashes. Some Middle Eastern children dress in costume on this day and collect treats, making the holiday similar to Halloween. One traditional dish, *Burbura* (Arabic for Barbara) is a pudding that includes shelled wheat and apricots, a reminder of what the patron saint of miners and firefighters had to eat when she was locked in the tower.

Arab American girls at an Islamic summer school in Pasadena, California, where all instruction is conducted in the Arabic language. Many immigrants from the Middle East consider it vital that they pass on their cultural traditions and native tongue to their children.

Islam in North America

The earliest Arab immigrants to the United States were Christian, but many who have come after 1965 are Muslim. Because neither the Census Bureau nor the Bureau of Citizenship and Immigration Services collects religious information in its data, it's difficult to determine the number of American Muslims. The estimates vary widely, from 2 million to 7 million. Indisputably, Islam is a fast-growing faith in the United States, and many of its converts are African American. The Institute of Islamic Information and Education (IIIE) estimates that by 2010, Islam will be the second-largest faith in the United States, after Christianity. The IIIE also estimates that 77.6 percent of American Muslims are immigrants, and that ethnically, about 36 percent of all American Muslims trace their heritage to the Middle East.

According to Gisela Webb's article "Expressions of Islam in America," some mosques take on a distinctive Western flavor. "Adaptations were made to conform to American church patterns, such as scheduling congregational prayers on Sundays and allowing 'mixed' (men and women) social functions, such as dances," she writes. These practices have been frowned upon by more recent Muslim arrivals, who tend to hold more conservative beliefs.

Webb says a conflict sometimes exists between certain Muslim practices and Western culture. "In general, Muslims in America who have been raised in traditional Muslim cultures speak of the tension they experience in trying to remain close to linguistic, cultural, ethnic, and religious roots while trying to develop a sense of belonging in their adopted home," she says. "Work schedules do not easily allow for the five-times-daily salat prayers or Friday congregational prayers. Institutional eating facilities (schools, prisons, military) are not set up for Muslim dietary practices. The pervasiveness of alcohol in America and the cultural acceptance of sexual permissiveness and immodesty . . . are seen as negative influences on the faith community, particularly on its young people."

And as Yvonne Yazbeck Haddad mentions in *A Community of Many Worlds: Arab Americans in New York City*, "They [Muslims] soon become aware that the public school system is geared to eradicate immigrant culture, and that it has generally been successful in this endeavor through long school days that incorporate co-educational activities such as swimming, dancing, acting, hobbies, and trips (which often violate Muslim desires for separation of the sexes)."

In June 2003, the *Sunday Star-Ledger* reported that the first brand-new Shiite mosque in the United States would be constructed in Franklin Township, New Jersey. While other Shiite mosques are in existence, they had previously been used for other purposes. The New Jersey mosque, which will also house a social hall and an Islamic elementary school, will be the center of worship for at least 300 Muslim families. The $3 million mosque will be a welcome change for Franklin Township's Muslims, who had been meeting in a house.

Language—Living or Lost

Many Arabic dialects, or regional language variations, exist in the Middle East—sometimes within the same country. It's understandable, then, that there are variations in the Arabic spoken by Arabs in North America. Take for example, the Arabic word *mabsoot*: Iraqis use it to mean physically beaten; to the Lebanese, it means happy. "Many Arabs simply cannot communicate with each other because they cannot understand each other's dialects. . . . For all, the common language is English," writes Yvonne Yazbeck Haddad in *A Community of Many Worlds: Arab Americans in New York City*.

Margaret Salome, a linguist, identifies three categories of immigrants who tend to retain their native tongue: those who are of lower socioeconomic status; those who live in minority neighborhoods with many other speakers of the language; and those with a great deal of ethnic pride. A Yemeni community in upstate New York that speaks primarily Arabic exemplifies the first category. "Members of that community became laborers with low levels of income and education. Therefore, the socio-economic homogeneity formerly shared in Yemen continues in the United States; it encourages isolation from mainstream America, and it makes it easier for members to retain language, culture, and traditions," observes Salome in *Food for Our Grandmothers: Writings by Arab-American and Arab-Canadian Feminists*.

There's a connection between the number of language speakers and the rate of retention: When many people are speaking the language at social events and in business circles, the tongue lives on. Salome points to the Cuban American community in Miami as an example. "You can spend your life in this community, go to work, run a business, and never speak English," she notes.

Salome interviewed the coordinator of an Arabic-language school in Seattle. "Members of the Arabic-language speaking community are committed to the school; it's part of a larger project involving the creation of an Arab culture center," she reports. "Community members believe a primary benefit for their children will be a sense of pride in Arabic culture and heritage."

For Berbers, retaining their mother tongue, Tamazight, is a way of preserving their culture, even if they are on foreign soil. The few thousand Berbers living in the United States are not generally located in one particular area, says Arezki Boudif, a researcher in chemistry and president of the Amazigh Cultural Association in America (ACAA). "Teaching our children our language and culture is not easy because we are so spread out," he says. So, ACAA members have multi-state events, like the celebration of the Berber spring, where traditional songs are sung and poetry is read. ACAA also maintains a multi-location resource center, sponsors concerts and seminars, publishes a newsletter, and even helps people acquire Berber music that's hard to find in the United States. A Tamazight correspondence course is being planned as well.

6 STEREOTYPES, DISCRIMINATION, AND OTHER PROBLEMS

Even before the September 11, 2001, terrorist attacks, some Middle Eastern immigrants—especially Muslims and Arabs—had experienced the sting of racism. A string of international incidents fed the image of Muslims and Arabs as violent, anti-Western and anti-American fanatics. A partial list of these incidents includes the murder, by Palestinian terrorists, of Israeli athletes at the 1972 Summer Olympics in Munich, West Germany; the Iran hostage crisis (1979 to 1981); the 1983 suicide truck-bomb attack on the barracks of U.S. Marine peacekeepers in Beirut, Lebanon, which killed 241 servicemen and was believed to have been carried out by the Iran-backed Islamist group Hezbollah; the 1985 hijacking of the Italian cruise ship *Achille Lauro*, during which Palestinian terrorists murdered a wheelchair-bound American Jew and dumped his body overboard; the 1988 bombing of a Pan Am jetliner over Lockerbie, Scotland, which claimed 270 lives and was linked to the Libyan government; the 1993 bombing of the World Trade Center by Islamic fundamentalists with links to al-Qaeda; and the al-Qaeda-sponsored bombings of American embassies in Kenya and Tanzania in 1998, which resulted in more than 200 deaths and 4,000 injuries. In the wake of these and other outrages, some Americans viewed Middle Easterners as a group with fear, distrust, and hostility—even though there is no evidence to

◄ A makeshift memorial of plastic flowers stands in front of the destroyed barracks of the U.S. Marine peacekeeping contingent in Beirut, Lebanon. In the early hours of October 23, 1983, a member of an Islamist terrorist group drove a truck laden with explosives into the building, killing 241 American servicemen as they slept.

suggest that significant numbers of Middle Eastern immigrants support the actions of violent extremists.

But stereotypes are often hard to dispel. And, in the opinion of some experts, harmful stereotypes of Arabs, Arab Americans, and Muslims have long been perpetuated in American popular culture. Media critic Jack G. Shaheen examined more than 900 motion pictures, from the early days of Hollywood to the present, for his book *Reel Bad Arabs: How Hollywood Vilifies a People*. Among the recurring stereotypes he noted were that Arabs are primitive and fanatical and place little value on human life. Shaheen, who is also the author of *The TV Arabs*, believes that on the small screen Arabs are stereotyped as "billionaires, bombers and belly dancers." But, he writes in *A Community of Many Worlds: Arab Americans in New York City*, what is most disturbing about television movies and programs with Arab characters "is that they effectively show all Arabs, Muslims, and Arab Americans as being at war with the United States."

Living in the Shadow of September 11

Not surprisingly, the terrorist acts of September 11, 2001, stirred powerful emotions among Americans. In the minds of a small number of people, the violence and pain inflicted on the victims and their families justified vigilante-style revenge against Arab and Muslim Americans. Between September 11, 2001, and October 1, 2001, the U.S. Commission on Civil Rights received 692 reports of ethnic intimidation; more than half were directed toward Arab Americans. Because of underreporting, the actual number of incidents may be significantly higher.

Hateful words and slashed tires were among the lesser offenses. An Indiana man repeatedly rammed his car into a mosque, and a Muslim woman wearing traditional headdress was punched while waiting for a bus. According to the Civil Rights Commission, she was asked, "Where are you going? To mosque, to bombing classes?" A Sikh gas station owner, mistaken for a Muslim, was shot and killed.

The hate crimes were widely condemned. The Civil Rights Commission ran a public service announcement encouraging tolerance, and several state governments organized public forums. David Shaheed, an Indiana judge, told the Civil Rights Commission, "These [hate] incidents were limited and merely a trifling annoyance compared to the outpouring of concern by leaders of government and the faith communities to see that Muslims and people of Middle Eastern appearance were not unjustly targeted for abuse and attack."

However, in the 11 months after the attacks, the U.S. Department of Justice detained hundreds of Middle Easterners on immigration violations such as overstaying their visas or entering the United States illegally, as the government sought to identify possible terrorists. Some detainees were held for eight months or more without being charged with a crime.

In the immediate aftermath of the September 11, 2001, attacks on the World Trade Center and Pentagon, Arab and Muslim Americans lived under a pall of suspicion.

A report by the Justice Department's Office of the Inspector General, released in June 2003, criticized the treatment of some detainees, saying they were physically and verbally abused by prison guards while being held in excessively harsh conditions—at times in maximum security, wearing leg shackles. The report acknowledged that the chaos and uncertainty that followed the attacks made the Justice Department's job more difficult, but it said not all of the abuses could be excused. The department stood by its policies as necessary to protect the country from further attacks.

In June 2002 the Bush administration announced what quickly became a controversial set of immigration regulations: the National Security Entry-Exit Registration System. Attorney General John Ashcroft said, "This system will expand substantially America's scrutiny of those foreign visitors who may pose a national security concern and enter our country. And it will provide a vital line of defense in the war against terrorism." The system, which went into effect on September 11, 2002, required male nationals and citizens from certain countries to

From Lost Boys to Found Men

Many Americans became aware of the long-running Sudanese civil war only after hearing about the plight of the Lost Boys of Sudan.

Fighting between the Sudanese military and the Sudan People's Liberation Army (SPLA) erupted in 1983; as of 2001, the war had led to the deaths of an estimated 2 million people. Many Sudanese children lost their parents or were separated from their families. By 1987 an estimated 20,000 young people, mostly boys from the Dinka and Nuer tribes, began a trek for survival, walking hundreds of miles in search of a safe haven from the fighting and, in many cases, for food. Many died during that quest; the luckier ones found their way to refugee camps, first in Ethiopia and later in Kenya. Although UNICEF has reunited some of the children with their families, others remain in a Kenyan refugee camp.

About 3,400 of the Lost Boys—many of them now young men—have settled in the United States, the result of a 1999 U.S.–United Nations agreement.

be fingerprinted, photographed, and registered with the U.S. government. Registration occurred in waves, with the first group called on being men from Iran, Iraq, Libya, Sudan, and Syria; the next group included men from Algeria, Bahrain, Lebanon, Morocco, Oman, Qatar, Tunisia, the United Arab Emirates, and Yemen; Saudi Arabian, Egyptian, Jordanian, and Kuwaiti men also were asked to register. (Men from certain non–Middle Eastern countries, such as North Korea and Pakistan, were also included in this registration.)

The new system's most controversial aspect became the detention of individuals who had pending applications with the immigration service, and the "call in" of many individuals for interviews at INS offices.

In June 2003, the Washington, D.C.–based Migration Policy Institute produced a report, with input from past Republican and Democratic INS commissioners, highly critical of a number of the immigration policies adopted after September 11. It criticized the "voluntary interview" program of Arabs and Muslims in the United States, noting, "The immigration enforcement focus [a number of people interviewed were detained] and public fanfare that surrounded the program worked against its potential for intelligence gathering." The report also stated that the "call-in special registration program has been poorly planned and has not achieved its objectives. Its goals have been contradictory: gathering information about non-immigrants [temporary visa holders] present in the United States, and deporting those with immigration violations. Many non-immigrants have rightly feared they will be detained or deported if they attempt to comply, so they have not registered. Moreover, any potential security benefits of registering people inside the United States will fade over time."

The report noted the "profound positive impact" of President Bush's visit to a Washington, D.C., mosque in the days after September 11. However, it also stated that many of the immigration-related measures taken have been "ineffective in responding to threats of terrorism, but are undertaken for political expediency or public relations at a huge price to" Arab and Muslim communities in the United States. The Migration Policy Institute report advocated greater emphasis on intelligence and information sharing and more cooperative engagement by law enforcement with Arab and Muslim communities.

In many cases, the government's search for terrorists has resulted in the deportation of individuals for minor violations of immigration law. In January 2003, the *Atlanta Journal-Constitution* reported that deportees included "an Arab student in New York who was expelled for working seven hours a week beyond what his visa allowed and a Jordanian in New Jersey who violated terms of a tourist visa by working at a Dunkin' Donuts." The newspaper's computer analysis of INS data revealed that deportations to some Middle Eastern, North African, and South Asian countries more than doubled from October 2001 to September 2002, while the number of Mexican deportees dropped by nearly 25 percent.

By spring 2003, the Bush administration ended the special registration program, purportedly because it had accomplished its mission. All told, 130,000 men registered, 11,000 were questioned, and more than 2,300 were detained.

Attitudes of Arab Americans

The September 11, 2001, attack on the United States by al-Qaeda has left its mark on the Arab American community. A May 2002 survey by Zogby International and the Arab American Institute Foundation, "Profiling and Pride: Arab American Attitudes and Behavior Since September 11," sheds light on how Arab Americans view themselves.

The survey sample of 505 randomly selected Arab Americans, three-fourths of whom were born in the United States, included Christians (63 percent), Muslims (24 percent), and those with other or no religious affiliation (13 percent). Of the respondents, 89 percent were very proud or extremely proud of their ethnicity, and 66 percent of those not born in the United States said their ties were very strong to their birth country. When asked whether ethnic heritage was important in defining themselves, about half of the total sample said it was very important; that percentage rose to about 70 percent among respondents not born in the United States.

The overwhelming majority of Arab Americans are peace-loving, law-abiding people who care about their adopted country. As the study concludes, most "reacted to the terrorist attacks

Living the First Amendment

In his homeland of Egypt, says Tamer Melek, a Coptic Christian, wearing a crucifix necklace or attending church can be a "big problem." Christians may suffer discrimination ranging from the subtle (for example, being passed over for job promotions in favor of Muslims) to the flagrant (such as verbal harassment or even violence).

"Copts don't get the best jobs," says Melek, who was relegated to a low-level position in the Egyptian army once officials learned he was Christian. (Egyptians carry an identification card that includes religious affiliation.) "My father saw many younger Muslims with less experience getting promoted. The police stand guard outside the churches. The Muslim neighbors notice, too. They'll ask why you don't pray with them."

Melek had always wanted to travel, but his father persuaded him to finish his education first. And so he earned his college degree and served in the army, but there was one final barrier keeping him from leaving Egypt: finances. "To apply for a visa, you have to have money in the bank, about $25,000," he explains. "I didn't have the money, but I went to my uncle, a businessman, and told him of my situation. Much to my surprise, he agreed to put the money in the bank for me."

When Melek came to New York in 1996, he had a cousin and an aunt already in the United States to help him get acclimated. He also had another "family": members of an Egyptian Coptic church. They helped him avoid the pitfalls of immigration, such as unscrupulous lawyers or scam artists who take an unsuspecting client's money but don't take the necessary steps to keep the person in the country legally.

The mere existence of a Coptic church, without police officers present or harassment from onlookers, is to Melek a welcome miracle. "I can wear a cross—no problem. No one asks me, 'Why are you going to church?'" he says. "Here I can do whatever I want, and there are no problems."

in the same ways that their fellow Americans did: by hanging flags, contributing to funds, and donating blood." Whether "mainstream" America will be able to grasp that fact will be clearer in the future. Still, about 40 percent of the survey's respondents said they knew someone who had been discriminated against since the attack; approximately one-fifth said they had personally experienced discrimination. Many Arab Americans are concerned about the long-term effects of discrimination.

All in the Family

External forces such as racism and discrimination may not be the only difficulties Middle Easterners in North America face. The vastly different nature of Western society may also engender more subtle internal tensions. These struggles often play out between generations of the family. In *Arabs in America: Building a New Future*, sociologist Kristine Ajrouch writes about Arabic-speaking, Muslim students in a middle school in

Koran class, Dearborn, Michigan. Uncomfortable with what they perceive as the permissiveness of North American society, many Arab immigrants, particularly Muslims, want their children to follow the gender norms that prevail in their countries of origin.

Dearborn, Michigan. Their parents, she notes, "are products of the traditional, agrarian culture of the Middle East, where the past is revered, there is emphasis on stability and conformity, and the elderly are held in high esteem because of their life experiences." By contrast, Ajrouch says, the children "are growing up in the technological, industrial culture of America. For them, the focus is on the future, not the past. Youth have higher status than the elderly, and emphasis is placed on personal achievement, rather than accumulated life experiences."

The Arab family has been described as patrilineal—that is, one where each member's rights and responsibilities are defined through the father. And yet, suggests Ajrouch, the family's honor pivots on the behavior of its female members, specifically their sexual conduct. "Chastity and honor," Ajrouch notes, "become imperative qualities for the female."

That being the case, it's not surprising that Arab young men are given a looser social rein than their sisters. A survey of Arab Canadian youth showed that even the younger generation adheres to traditional Arab attitudes toward women. Both teen males and teen females were asked to rate certain behaviors as favorable, unfavorable, or neutral. A young Arab man going out on dates, for example, was viewed as favorable by 62 percent of males and 53 percent of females. But a young Arab woman going out on dates was considered favorable by only 28 percent of males and 44 percent of females.

"The fact that dating and having a boyfriend or a girlfriend is considered normal and even desirable in American society prompts Arab parents to maintain a stronger hold on their daughters," writes Ajrouch. However, "the same standards and expectations that are levied on Arab girls are not applied to the non-Arab girls that the boys date."

For some Middle Eastern parents, the "anything goes" Western culture is just too much to handle. "Quite a number of Iranian parents have left this country because of their anxieties in raising their daughters in a culture with permissive sexual attitudes," writes Ali Akbar Mahdi in "The Second Generation

Iranians: Questions and Concerns." "Some second generation youth," he adds, "are torn between trying to be what their parents want them to be and what the American society wants them to be. For some, these choices involve betrayal and ostracism, and a happy medium is hard, if not impossible, to achieve."

Middle Eastern American and Canadian immigrants tend to be stricter parents than is the Western norm, but that alone doesn't tell the whole family story. These families often spend a great deal of time together, with the mother spending the most time with her children. In the Arab Canadian teen survey, 69 percent of sons and 63 percent of daughters said they spent a considerable amount of time with their moms; only 59 percent of boys and 28 percent of girls said they spent a considerable amount of time with their dads. And even though much of these parent-child activities involved working around the house or shopping, about one-third of both male and female respondents said they wanted to spend more time with their parents. The Arab Canadian teens felt close to at least one parent; 9 of 10 who took the survey said they confided personally in their mother, father, or both parents.

Americans with an Eye on Their Birthplace

Not all Middle Easterners who come to North America intend to make Canada or the United States their permanent home. Some complete their education and return to their homeland. Others wait for a stronger economy or for a more peaceful period in their country. Still others decide that the Western lifestyle clashes too much with their religious or cultural values.

John, a Sudanese refugee, was interviewed by Rogaia Mustafa Abusharaf, who said he described his experiences as "someone who is unexpectedly stranded away from home." At the time of the interview, John, who earned his Ph.D. in the United States, did not have a full-time job but was sending part of his salary to family in Sudan. He said, "I would like to go back to the Sudan once peace [and] racial, religious, and cultural equality is established. Because life here is not problem-free. Loneliness, stress, and racism are the most common problems."

Undocumented Immigrants and Refugees

In the United States, legal immigrants—foreign-born people who seek the right to live and work in the country permanently and have the proper documentation—must obtain a green card, or permanent resident visa. Green cards are issued by the Bureau of Citizenship and Immigration Services. A permanent resident need not seek to become an American citizen if he or she does not wish to. Compared with immigrants from other parts of the world, Middle Eastern immigrants have a higher U.S. citizenship rate than immigrants overall.

Not all foreign-born people living within U.S. borders are doing so legally. Estimates of the number of people in the United States illegally in 2003 ranged up to 8 million. These people have entered the country without official documentation or permission, stayed longer in the country than their temporary visas allowed (referred to in immigration circles as "overstays"), or violated the terms of their visas (for example, by taking a job while in the country on a tourist visa). It's difficult to get a precise count of undocumented immigrants because, to state the obvious, few want to make their status known and risk deportation. However, based on government statistics, estimates of the number of Middle Easterners living in the United States illegally range from 100,000 to 200,000; Iran, Lebanon, and Jordan were among the top five source countries, according to U.S. government data.

The tougher stance on immigration that the United States adopted after September 11 drove many Middle Easterners living illegally in the United States to the Canadian border. Most were trying to beat the INS-imposed registration deadline for men from 25 Middle Eastern countries. They sought refugee status in Canada.

The U.S. Refugee Act of 1980 defines a refugee as "a person outside of his or her country of nationality who is unable or unwilling to return because of persecution or a well-founded fear of persecution on account of race, religion, nationality, membership in a particular social group, or political opinion." There are close to 15 million refugees and asylum seekers worldwide; in the Middle East alone, there are roughly 6.8 million refugees, many of them Palestinians or Afghanis, according to the World Refugee Survey 2002.

The United States is host to about 500,000 refugees, most of whom are from Central American nations such as El Salvador and Guatemala. Middle Eastern refugees who are resettled in the United States include former Iraqi soldiers, Chaldeans, and Kurds.

Life in their new country, especially at first, can be difficult. In her article "Meet Your Brother with a Welcoming Smile—Refugees in America," Anne Marie Weiss-Armush writes about a Turkish Kurd refugee, Rukeiya, who came to the United States in 1992:

> I found Rukeiya and her six small children huddled in the corner of a dark, dank apartment not far from my well-manicured neighborhood in North Dallas. Other than the bundles she carried from her previous home in a Turkish mountain camp she had received only a few mattresses, eight dishes and spoons, and a single set of small American cooking pots. . . . [Her] husband, Ahmed, was taken by public transportation to a minimum wage night job, where he cleaned buses. As the family had been registered for food stamps and the children enrolled at school, the sponsoring agency closed its file.

Although life as a refugee is rarely easy, for many Middle Eastern refugees, the hardships are an improvement over the persecution they suffered in their own country. In several Middle Eastern Muslim countries, Christians can be imprisoned, forced into slavery, or killed for their beliefs. Seeking refugee status, not an easy process to begin with, was made more difficult for some Middle Easterners after September 11,

2001. Many refugees from Muslim countries found that U.S. security procedures added after the terrorist attacks created such delays that they found themselves still in refugee camps more than a year after having been approved for refugee status in the United States.

Refugees in Canada

Canada's Immigration and Refugee Protection Act of 2002 enables people to be given refugee status through a resettlement program, in which they are brought from other countries and have Canadian government assistance or private sponsors; or, for individuals already in the country, through a refugee claim process. In 2001, there were nearly 28,000 refugees in Canada. Once they have lived in Canada for three years, refugees can apply for Canadian citizenship.

7 An Uncertain Future

Middle Easterners have been immigrating to the United States for more than a century. In 2000, according to the U.S. census, there were an estimated 1.5 million Middle Eastern immigrants in the United States, and the Center for Immigration Studies predicted that, in the absence of changes to U.S. immigration policy, an additional 1.1 million would arrive between 2001 and 2010.

Historically, though, U.S. immigration policy (and the treatment of certain ethnic groups) has been shaped by world events. In the aftermath of World War I, for example, an increasingly isolationist United States shut its doors to many immigrants with the development and passage of the Immigration Act of 1924, which imposed strict numerical quotas on certain nationalities. During the Great Depression, immigration was further limited when the State Department ordered consular officials to deny visas to all prospective immigrants who might at any time be unable to support themselves. After Japan's bombing of the U.S. naval base at Pearl Harbor, Hawaii, in December 1941, thousands of Japanese Americans on the West Coast were removed from their homes and taken to internment camps. More recently, some of the immigration reforms following September 11, such as the registration of men from certain countries, directly affected Middle Easterners.

◀ After more than a century of immigration to Canada and the United States, Middle Easterners have become an integral part of multicultural North America.

A Few Scenarios

A second al-Qaeda-orchestrated attack on American soil would certainly affect public opinion, and it might also influence public policy. Most likely, Middle Easterners would have a more difficult time rejoining family members who had already immigrated, earning a college degree in the United States, or pursuing the American Dream.

Another development that might have a potentially major effect on Middle Eastern immigration to the United States would be the resolution of the Israeli-Palestinian conflict and the establishment of an independent Palestinian state. In the wake of the war in Iraq that ousted Saddam Hussein in 2003, the Bush administration promoted its peace plan for Israel and the Palestinians, dubbed the "road map." The plan called for the establishment of an independent Palestinian state within a few years, although continued Israeli-Palestinian violence made that outcome uncertain. If a Palestinian state were created, however, the result might well be a significant reduction in the number of Palestinians seeking to immigrate to North America. In addition, just as Jews from all over the world flocked to Israel following the creation of the Jewish state in 1948, many Palestinians living abroad—including those in Canada and the United States—might leave to help build up the new country.

Consider some other scenarios. What if the Berber language and culture were able to flourish in Algeria, where Berbers seeking to retain their traditions have been at the center of recurring civil unrest? Or if the Coptic Christians were no longer discriminated against in Egypt? It's possible these people would still come to North America to be reunited with family or go to college. But the push factors of migration would almost certainly be diminished, resulting in fewer immigrants from that part of the world.

For some Middle Easterners, the doors to North America might already be closing. For example, aside from asylum and refugee claims and the Diversity Lottery (which is at best a long shot), few options are available to the Sudanese, as

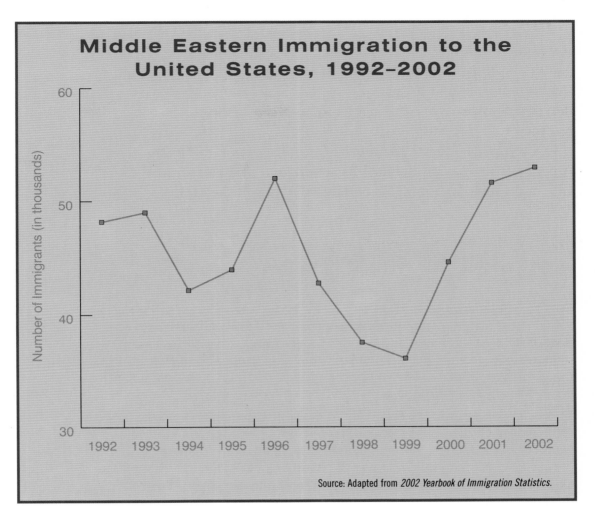

Middle Eastern Immigration to the United States, 1992–2002

Number of Immigrants (in thousands)

60

50

40

30

1992 1993 1994 1995 1996 1997 1998 1999 2000 2001 2002

Source: Adapted from *2002 Yearbook of Immigration Statistics.*

Middle Eastern immigration to the United States increased by about 40 percent between 1998 and 2002, reaching a 10-year high. But the long-term effects of the September 11, 2001, terrorist attacks on immigration remain unclear.

Rogaia Mustafa Abusharaf explains. "Entering the United States is extremely difficult, especially since the closing of the American and Canadian consulates in Khartoum," she notes. "This difficulty is likely to persist."

Even Canada, which has earned a reputation as a haven for immigrants, might not be as welcoming in the future. Some Canadians, according to an article in the January 2003 issue of *Migration News*, have suggested that the country is accepting too many immigrants. And the ripple effects of September 11 extend northward.

"The high percentage of persons of Middle Eastern origin among Canadian immigrants and especially refugees," the

Migration News story notes, "has increased tensions with the U.S. government, which believes that some Canadians from the Middle East have terrorist links. . . . Since June 2002, under the Immigration and Refugee Protection Regulations, most asylum seekers who arrive in Canada by the way of the U.S. are returned to request asylum."

To varying degrees, the number of people coming to North America from the Middle East has continued to increase since U.S. and Canadian immigration laws changed in the 1960s.

A Rainbow After a Storm

The days and weeks after September 11, 2001, were frightening for all Americans, but uniquely for foreign-born Arab Muslim Americans. The possibility of hate crimes and the U.S. government's registration requirement for men from Muslim countries generated tremendous concern. But like a rainbow after a storm, a hope for better understanding of Muslim Americans has emerged at one Maryland college.

After 9/11, Hoda Zaki, an Egyptian immigrant and a political science professor at Hood College, found herself in an unusual situation. She was a nominal Muslim who identified more as an Arab American and a person of color than as a follower of Islam. In fact, Zaki came to the United States to pursue a master's degree at a traditionally African American college. "The Arab Americans I knew were part of an 'invisible' community that tried to blend in with the mainstream. I distanced myself from them, but connected with the African American community, where I felt welcome," says Zaki, director of Hood's African American Studies program.

Then came 9/11 and its aftermath. "The college was holding an interdenominational prayer service, and the chaplain asked if I would read from the Koran," says Zaki. "I was unsure at first, as being Muslim was not a strong part of my identity, but being Arab American was."

Nonetheless, Zaki took part in the service. Her participation led a small, previously non-vocal group of international Muslim students to ask her if she'd be the adviser for a newly formed Muslim Student Association. She said yes, and the result has been a student organization that's opened new channels of communication at Hood College. "I'm heartened by this movement, by which the entire campus has been enriched," says Zaki.

(One notable exception: Because of the Islamic Revolution in 1979, immigration from Iran dramatically spiked during the 1980s, but then dropped to only slightly above pre-revolution levels the following decade.)

The course of Middle Eastern immigration is difficult to predict. The war on terrorism, U.S. immigration policy, and the prospects for peace in the region all will affect the outlook for future immigration from the Middle East.

FAMOUS MIDDLE EASTERN AMERICANS/CANADIANS

Middle Easterners have been coming to North America since the late 1800s, so there are many famous Americans today who claim that heritage: Spencer Abraham, George W. Bush's secretary of energy; football player Doug Flutie; the founder of Mothers Against Drunk Driving, Candy Lightner; the founder of Kinko's copying stores, Paul Orfalea; rock legend Frank Zappa; actor Tony Shalhoub; poet Naomi Shihab Nye; consumer advocate and activist Ralph Nader; and many more. Listed below are some well-known Middle Eastern immigrants who have come to North America since 1965.

Christiane Amanpour, journalist. The award-winning CNN correspondent was born in London, but her family moved to Iran when she was an infant. In 1979 Amanpour's family came to the United States because of the Islamic Revolution. Amanpour has earned many accolades, particularly for her war reporting.

Amin Barakat, physician. Dr. Barakat, who received the Ellis Island Medal of Honor in 2000, is a world-renowned pediatrician. His specialty is the treatment of children with kidney disease. The doctor and his family immigrated in 1986 because of the civil war in his homeland, Lebanon.

Manute Bol, basketball player. An NBA basketball player for 11 years and a Sudanese Dinka tribesman, Bol returned to Sudan for a few years but has come back to the United States. He established the Ring True Foundation to help Sudan's "Lost Boys."

Fawaz Ismail, entrepreneur. Ismail, who is of Palestinian descent, is the founder and president of Alamo Flag Company. The company is the largest distributor of American flags in the United States. He immigrated to the United States when he was nine years old.

Bijan Mortazavi, violinist. Born in Iran, the versatile musician attended college at Texas State University in 1979 and settled in California in 1985. Mortazavi has performed in concert halls worldwide, including New York's Lincoln Center.

The Iron Sheik, wrestler. An Olympic gold medalist in wrestling while representing Iran, the Iron Sheik (birth name: Khosrow Vaziri) came to the United States in 1970. For many years he was one of the World Wrestling Foundation's stars.

assimilation: a process by which a person from one culture takes on the mind-set, habits, and customs of another culture.

Diaspora: the community of Jews living outside Palestine.

emigration: the act of leaving one country to settle in another.

first generation: people born in one country who move to another.

hate crimes: violent or destructive acts committed against a person or property because of ethnicity, sexual orientation, or physical disabilities.

Koran: the holy book of Islam; also spelled Qur'an.

legal immigrants: people who want to become permanent residents of a country outside the country of their birth and have the proper documentation.

monotheistic: believing in one God.

1.5 generation: a term sometimes used to refer to people who immigrated to the United States as children (usually when their parents immigrated).

overstays: foreigners who remain in the United States longer than their visa permits.

pull factors: characteristics of, or situations in, a particular country (for example, civil liberties, employment or educational opportunities, the presence of family members) that attract prospective immigrants to that country.

push factors: characteristics of, or situations in, a country (for example, civil war, religious or political persecution, poverty, famine) that make people want to leave that country.

refugee: a person outside of his or her country of origin who is unable or unwilling to return because of persecution or a well-founded fear of persecution on account of race, religion, nationality, membership in a particular social group, or political opinion.

second generation: the children of immigrants born in the country to which their parents immigrated.

FURTHER READING

Abraham, Nabeel, and Andrew Shryock, eds. *Arab Detroit: From Margin to Mainstream.* Detroit: Wayne State University Press, 2000.

Abusharaf, Rogaia Mustafa. *Wanderings: Sudanese Migrants and Exiles in North America.* Ithaca, N.Y.: Cornell University Press, 2002.

Ansari, Sarah, and Vanessa Martin, eds. *Women, Religion, and Culture in Iran.* London: Curzon Press, 2001.

Asayesh, Gelareh. *Saffron Sky: A Life Between Iran and America.* Boston: Beacon Press, 1999.

Benson, Kathleen, and Philip M. Kayal, eds. *A Community of Many Worlds: Arab Americans in New York City.* New York: Museum of the City of New York/Syracuse University Press, 2002.

Chishti, Muzaffar A., et al. *America's Challenge: Domestic Security, Civil Liberties, and National Unity After September 11.* Washington, D.C.: Migration Policy Institute, 2003.

Kadi, Joanna, ed. *Food for Our Grandmothers: Writings by Arab-American and Arab-Canadian Feminists.* Boston: South End Press, 1994.

Sabar, Naama. *Kibbutzniks in the Diaspora.* Albany: State University of New York Press, 2000.

Suleiman, Michael W., ed. *Arabs in America: Building a New Future.* Philadelphia: Temple University Press, 1999.

INTERNET RESOURCES

http://menic.utexas.edu/menic/

The Middle East Network Information Center, or MENIC, is a public service of the Center for Middle Eastern Studies at the University of Texas-Austin. Maps, historical records, country profiles, and governmental and cultural information are part of this comprehensive site.

http://www.freep.com/jobspage/arabs/

The *Detroit Free Press* serves the country's largest population of Arab Americans. The newspaper developed "100 Questions and Answers About Arab Americans" primarily for journalists, but anyone can benefit from the site's "frequently asked questions" about Arab American origins, language, demographics, family issues, customs, religion, and politics.

http://www.aaiusa.org

Since 1985 the Arab American Institute has encouraged political and civic participation by Americans of Arab descent and served as a clearinghouse of information about the Arab American community. This site provides demographic and census information about Arab Americans and tackles the hot policy issues surrounding the community. An online quiz tests the participant's knowledge about Arab Americans.

http://www.islamonline.net

A comprehensive source about Islam, this site includes relevant articles about health and science, art and entertainment, and other contemporary issues. It is designed for non-Muslims as well as Muslims.

http://i-cias.com/e.o

From Abadan to Zurvanism, the Encyclopedia of the Orient has a wealth of information about North Africa and the Middle East.

Publisher's Note: The websites listed on this page were active at the time of publication. The publisher is not responsible for websites that have changed their address or discontinued operation since the date of publication. The publisher reviews and updates the websites each time the book is reprinted.

Index

1965 Immigration Act, 18
1976 Immigration Act (Canada), 49
1952 Immigration and Nationality Act, 40
1965 Immigration and Nationality Act, 40–41, 58

Abu-Laban, Baha, 58
Abu-Laban, Sharon McIrvin, 58
Abusharaf, Rogaia Mustafa, 55–56, 92–93, 99
Ajrouch, Kristine, 90–91
Alexander the Great, 23, 24
Algeria, 31, 32, 35
bin Ali, Sharif Hussein, 28
    See also Ottoman Empire
Amanpour, Christiane, 102
Amazigh Cultural Association in America (ACAA), 81
Arab American Institute Foundation, 18, 61, 88
Arab American National Museum, 66
Arab Americans, 18
    assimilation, 69–70, 72–75
    communities, 61–64
    culture, 74, 76–79
    discrimination, 43, **44**, 83–90
    education, 64, 75
    organizations, 64, 66–67
    population, 19–20, 61, 97
Arab Community Center for Economic and Social Services (ACCESS), 64, 66
    See also organizations
Arabs in America (Suleiman), 18, 51, 58, 69, 70, 90–91
Arian, Asher, 54, 55
Asayesh, Gelareh, 59, 77–78
Ashcroft, John, 86
assimilation, 69–70, 72–75
    See also Arab Americans
"Awareness! What Does it Take?" (Mounir), 20

Bahrain, 32, 51
Bar Kochba Rebellion, 24, 54
    See also history, Middle Eastern
Barakat, Amin, 102
Blue Mosque, **27**
Bol, Manute, 102
Boudif, Arezki, 81
"Browner Shades of White" (Halaby), 20
Bureau of Citizenship and Immigration Services (BCIS), 19, 43
Bureau of Customs and Border Protection (BCBP), 43
Bureau of Immigration and Customs Enforcement (BICE), 43
Bush, George W., **42**, 87, 88, 98

Cainker, Louise, 51–52, 54
Canada, 93–94, 95, 99–100
    immigration history, 18, 46, 48–49
    immigration rates, 58–59
    population, Middle Eastern immigrant, 19–20, 71
Chinese Exclusion Act of 1882, 37, **38**
    See also ethnicity
Christianity, 24–25, 26, 30–31, 55, 56–57, 78, 89, 94
    See also religion
Citizenship and Immigration Canada, 19
civil war, 31, **56**, 87
Coderre, Denis, 58, 59
Cohen, Rina, 69
communities, 61–64, **90**, 91
    See also Arab Americans
A Community of Many Worlds (Benson and Kayal), 62–63, 74–75, 80, 84
Crusades, 24, 26
    See also history, Middle Eastern
culture, 74, 76–80
    See also Arab Americans

Dearborn, Mich., 61–62, **90**, 91
Delights from the Garden of Eden (Nasrallah), 65
Department of Homeland Security, 43
    See also Immigration and Naturalization Service (INS)

Numbers in **bold italic** refer to captions.

discrimination, 43, *44*, 83–90
Displaced Persons Act of 1948, 39–40
   See also refugees
diversity lottery. *See* visas
Druze, 31
   See also religion

Egypt, 32, 35
Ellis Island, *37*
Enhanced Border Security and Visa
   Entry Reform Act (2002), 42–43
ethnicity, 15, 18, 20, 29, 37, *38*, 46, 57,
   58, 97
"Expressions of Islam in America"
   (Webb), 66–67, 79

family structure, *69*, 90–92
   See also culture
Fermi, Laura, 39
Food for Our Grandmothers (Kadi),
   80–81
France, *28*, 29

gender roles, 75–76, 91
Grant, Madison, 39
Great Britain, 28–29
Gulf War (1991), 52–53, 65
   See also Iraq

Haddad, Yvonne Yazbeck, 74, 80
Hajar, Paula, 75
Halaby, Laila, 20
history, Middle Eastern, 23–31, 35
The History of Arab Immigration to the
   U.S. (Cainker), 51–52
holidays, 77–78
   See also culture
Homeland Security Act of 2002, 43
Hungarian Revolution (1956), 48
Hussein, Saddam, 29, 52, 98

illegal immigrants. *See* undocumented
   immigrants
Illegal Immigration Reform and Immigrant
   Responsibility Act (1996), 42

immigration
   attitudes toward, 38
   difficulties of, 69–70, 72–75, 94, 98–99
   history of, in Canada, 18, 46, 48–49
   history of, in the United States, 18,
      37–45, 97
   rates of, in Canada, 58–59
   rates of, in the United States, 37,
      39–40, 44, 52–53, *66*, *99*
   reasons for, 21, 49–57
Immigration Act of 1924, 39, 97
   See also quotas
Immigration Act of 1965, 18
Immigration Act of 1990, 42
Immigration Act of 1952 (Canada), 48
Immigration and Nationality Act (1952),
   40
Immigration and Nationality Act of 1965,
   40–41, 58
Immigration and Naturalization Service
   (INS), 19, 41, 43
Immigration and Refugee Protection Act
   (Canada), 49, 95
Immigration Reform and Control Act
   (1986), 42
Institute of Islamic Information and
   Education (IIIE), 78
Iran, 15, 19, 26, 30, 32, 35, *66*, 75–76, 101
Iraq, 26, 29, 30–31, 32, 52–53, 65
Iron Sheik, 102
Islam, 23, 25–26, 30, 57, 72, 75–76,
   79–80, 90
   See also religion
Islamic Revolution (1979), 63, *66*, 101
   See also Iran
Ismail, Fawaz, 102
Israel, 30, 31, 32, 50, 53–55, 75
   See also Palestinian-Israeli conflict
Israeli-Palestinian conflict. *See*
   Palestinian-Israeli conflict
"Israelis in a Jewish Diaspora" (Lahav
   and Arian), 54

Jarrah, Mamoon, 47
Jarrah, Samar, 47

INDEX

Jerusalem, 24, 26, **53**
Johnson, Lyndon B., **41**
Jordan, 32, 35, 50
Journal of the International Institute, 62
Judaism, 23–24, 26, 30–31, 62–63,
    69–70
      See also religion

Kibbutzniks in the Diaspora (Sabar),
    54–55, 70
Kurds, 29, 52
    See also ethnicity
Kuwait, 30, 32, 35, 76

bin Laden, Osama, 21
    See also terrorism
Lahav, Gallya, 54, 55
language, 80–81
    See also culture
Laughlin, Harry N., 39
League of Nations, 28, 29
Lebanon, 29, 31, 33, 50
Libya, 33, 35
Los Angeles, 61, 63–64, 70
Lost Boys, 86
    See also Sudan

Mahdi, Ali Akbar, 72–73, 76, 91–92
Majaj, Lisa Suhair, 18
mandates, League of Nations, **28**, 29
    See also history, Middle Eastern
map, Middle East, **16–17**, **28**
Marcus, Scott, 74
"Meet Your Brother with a Welcoming
    Smile" (Weiss-Armush), 94
Melek, Tamer, 89
Mesopotamia. *See* Iraq
Middle East
    countries in, 15, 32–34
    history, 23–31, 35
    map, **16–17**, **28**
Middle East Quarterly, 57
Migration News, 99–100
Migration Policy Institute, 87–88
Morocco, 33, 35
Mortazavi, Bijan, 102

Mounir, Najat, 20
Muhammad, 25, 26, 30
    See also Islam
Muslims. *See* Islam
Mustafa, Naheed, 76
Mustafa, Shakir, 65
"My Body Is My Own Business"
    (Mustafa), 76

Nasrallah, Nawal, 65
National Security Entry-Exit Registration
    System, 86–88
      See also terrorism
"The New Immigrants" (Cohen), 69
New York City, 61, 62
Nicaraguan and Central American Relief
    Act, 58
      See also visas

Oman, 33, 51
organizations, 64, 66–67
    See also Arab Americans
Ottoman Empire, 26–29
    See also history, Middle Eastern

Palestine, 24, 28, 29, 53, 70
    See also Palestinian-Israeli conflict
Palestinian-Israeli conflict, 26, 29–30, **35**,
    47, **50**, 53–55, 98
Pearson, Lester, **46**, 48
points system, 48–49
    See also Canada
population
    Arab American, 19–20, 61, 97
    Middle Eastern immigrants, in
      Canada, 19–20, 71
push and pull immigration factors,
    49–53, 54–55
      See also immigration

al-Qaddafi, Muammar, 35
al-Qaeda, 21, 83, 88
    See also terrorism
Qatar, 33, 51
quotas, 21, 38–39, 40, **41**, 48, 97

Reel Bad Arabs (Shaheen), 84
Refugee Act of 1980, 41, 94
refugees, 39–40, 41, 45, 47, 48, 92–95, 99–100
religion, 15, 23–26, 29, 30–31, 50, 51, 55, 56–57, 66–67, 77–80, 89, 94
Rignall, Karen, 62
Roman Empire, 23–25
   See also history, Middle Eastern
Rose, Alexander, 57

Sabar, Naama, 54–55, 70
Saffron Sky (Asayesh), 59, 77–78
Salome, Margaret, 80–81
Samhan, Helen Hatab, 18
Saudi Arabia, 33, 35, 76
Scully, C. D., 38
"The Second Generation Iranians" (Mahdi), 72–73, 91–92
Seikaly, May, 70
September 11 attacks, 21, 43, 83, 84–85, 88, **99**, 100
   See also terrorism
Shaheed, David, 85
Shaheen, Jack G., 84
Shia Islam, 25–26, 29, 30, 52
   See also Islam
Sudan, 31, 33, 55–57, 86
Suleiman, Michael W., 51, 69
Süleyman the Magnificent, 27
   See also Ottoman Empire
Sultan Hassan Mosque, **23**
Sunni Islam, 25–26, 29, 30
   See also Islam
Syria, 29, 33, 50, 51

Temporary Quota Act of 1921, 39
   See also quotas
terrorism, 21, 43, 83–91, **99**, 100
Toronto, Ontario, 61
Treaty of Sèvres, 29
Tunisia, 34
Turkey, 15, 29, 31, 34, 75
   See also Ottoman Empire

undocumented immigrants, 42, 43, 45, 93–94
United Arab Emirates, 34
United States
   Arab American population, 19–20, 61, 97
   immigration history, 18, 37–45, 97
   immigration rates, 37, 39–40, 44, 52–53, **66**, **99**
      See also Arab Americans
USA PATRIOT Act (2002), 42

visas, 21, 38, 41, **44**
   diversity, 45, 57–58, 98

Wanderings (Abusharaf), 55–56
Washington Report on Middle East Affairs, 64
Wasp, 38
Webb, Gisela, 66–67, 79
Weiss-Armush, Anne Marie, 94
West Bank and Gaza Strip, 34, **35**
   See also Palestine
World War I, 27–29, 38–39, 97
World War II, 30, 38

Yemen, 34, 76
Yokich, Stephen, 64

Zaki, Hoda, 100
Zenner, Walter P., 62–63

CONTRIBUTORS

SENATOR EDWARD M. KENNEDY has represented Massachusetts in the United States Senate for more than forty years. Kennedy serves on the Senate Judiciary Committee, where he is the senior Democrat on the Immigration Subcommittee. He currently is the ranking member on the Health, Education, Labor and Pensions Committee in the Senate, and also serves on the Armed Services Committee, where he is a member of the Senate Arms Control Observer Group. He is also a member of the Congressional Friends of Ireland and a trustee of the John F. Kennedy Center for the Performing Arts in Washington, D.C.

Throughout his career, Kennedy has fought for issues that benefit the citizens of Massachusetts and the nation, including the effort to bring quality health care to every American, education reform, raising the minimum wage, defending the rights of workers and their families, strengthening the civil rights laws, assisting individuals with disabilities, fighting for cleaner water and cleaner air, and protecting and strengthening Social Security and Medicare for senior citizens.

Kennedy is the youngest of nine children of Joseph P. and Rose Fitzgerald Kennedy, and is a graduate of Harvard University and the University of Virginia Law School. His home is in Hyannis Port, Massachusetts, where he lives with his wife, Victoria Reggie Kennedy, and children, Curran and Caroline. He also has three grown children, Kara, Edward Jr., and Patrick, and four grandchildren.

Senior consulting editor STUART ANDERSON served as Executive Associate Commissioner for Policy and Planning and Counselor to the Commissioner at the Immigration and Naturalization Service from August 2001 until January 2003. He spent four and a half years on Capitol Hill on the Senate Immigration Subcommittee, first for Senator Spencer Abraham and then as Staff Director of the subcommittee for Senator Sam Brownback. Prior to that, he was Director of Trade and Immigration Studies at the Cato Institute in Washington, D.C., where he produced reports on the history of immigrants in the military and the role of immigrants in high technology. He currently serves as Executive Director of the National Foundation for American Policy, a nonpartisan public policy research organization focused on trade, immigration, and international relations. He has an M.A. from Georgetown University and a B.A. in Political Science from Drew University. His articles have appeared in such publications as the *Wall Street Journal*, *New York Times*, and *Los Angeles Times*.

MARIAN L. SMITH served as the senior historian of the U.S. Immigration and Naturalization Service (INS) from 1988 to 2003, and is currently the immigration and naturalization historian within the Department of Homeland Security in Washington, D.C. She studies, publishes, and speaks on the history of the immigration agency and is active in management of official 20th-century immigration records.

PETER HAMMERSCHMIDT is the First Secretary (Financial and Military Affairs) for the Permanent Mission of Canada to the United Nations. Before taking this position, he was a ministerial speechwriter and policy specialist for the Department of National

CONTRIBUTORS

Defence in Ottawa. Prior to joining the public service, he served as the Publications Director for the Canadian Institute of Strategic Studies in Toronto. He has a B.A. (Honours) in Political Studies from Queen's University, and an MScEcon in Strategic Studies from the University of Wales, Aberystwyth. He currently lives in New York, where in his spare time he operates a freelance editing and writing service, Wordschmidt Communications.

Manuscript reviewer ESTHER OLAVARRIA serves as General Counsel to Senator Edward M. Kennedy, ranking Democrat on the U.S. Senate Judiciary Committee, Subcommittee on Immigration. She is Senator Kennedy's primary advisor on immigration, nationality, and refugee legislation and policies. Prior to her current job, she practiced immigration law in Miami, Florida, working at several non-profit organizations. She cofounded the Florida Immigrant Advocacy Center and served as managing attorney, supervising the direct service work of the organization and assisting in the advocacy work. She also worked at Legal Services of Greater Miami, as the directing attorney of the American Immigration Lawyers Association Pro Bono Project, and at the Haitian Refugee Center, as a staff attorney. She clerked for a Florida state appellate court after graduating from the University of Florida Law School. She was born in Havana, Cuba, and raised in Florida.

Reviewer JANICE V. KAGUYUTAN is Senator Edward M. Kennedy's advisor on immigration, nationality, and refugee legislation and policies. Prior to working on Capitol Hill, Ms. Kaguyutan was a staff attorney at the NOW Legal Defense and Education Fund's Immigrant Women Program. Ms. Kaguyutan has written and trained extensively on the rights of immigrant victims of domestic violence, sexual assault, and human trafficking. Her previous work includes representing battered immigrant women in civil protection order, child support, divorce, and custody hearings, as well as representing immigrants before the Immigration and Naturalization Service on a variety of immigration matters.

SHEILA SMITH NOONAN is a writer from New Jersey. She has a B.A. in political science and journalism and graduated with honors from Douglass College, Rutgers University.

PICTURE CREDITS

Chapter Icon: PhotoDisc, Inc.
3: IMS Communications
14: Tom Nebbia/Corbis
16–17: © OTTN Publishing
19: Stephen Ferry/Liaison/Getty
Images
22: Corbis Images
24: Réunion des Musées
Nationaux/Art Resource,
NY
27: Turkish Embassy
28: © OTTN Publishing
35: Quique Kierszenbaum/Getty
Images
36: Hulton/Archive/Getty
Images
38: Library of Congress, Prints
and Photographs Division
[Reproduction Number
276]
41: Lyndon B. Johnson
Presidential Library
42: Alex Wong/Getty Images

44: AFP/Corbis
46: Hulton/Archive/Getty Images
50: Hulton/Archive/Getty Images
52: Hulton/Archive/Getty Images
53: Reuters NewMedia Inc./Corbis
56: Mario Tama/Getty Images
59: Reuters NewMedia Inc./Corbis
60: Ed Kashi/Corbis
63: PhotoDisc, Inc.
66: © OTTN Publishing
68: Ed Kashi/Corbis
71: © OTTN Publishing
72: PhotoDisc, Inc.
77: Corel Corporation
78: David Butow/Corbis Saba
82: Corbis
85: Mohammed Abed/AFP/Getty
Images
90: Ed Kashi/Corbis
96: Stephen Ferry/Liaison/Getty
Images
99: © OTTN Publishing

Cover: (front) AFP/Corbis; (back) Rabih Moghrabi/AFP/Getty Images

WITHDRAWN